# SAFE SEX

# SAFE SEX

## A Doctor Examines the Realities of AIDS and Other STDs

Joe S. McIlhaney, Jr., M.D.

**BAKER BOOK HOUSE**
Grand Rapids, Michigan 49516

# Contents

# Acknowledgments

Several people used their skills in the production of this book:

**Susan Nethery** did the initial editing and helped to shape the structure.

**Charlotte Matthews** patiently typed the drafts and revisions of the chapters and simplified the complexities of preparing the finished manuscript.

**John Dietrich, M.D.,** an infectious disease specialist, read the drafts and offered data to strengthen the presentations.

**Marion McIlhaney,** my wife, made many perceptive comments and continued to encourage me as the book developed.

PART

# STD—
# Singles and Sexuality

# STD
# Then and Now*

| | |
|---|---|
| *Before 1960* | **Syphilis and gonorrhea**<br>The only major STDs. |
| *1976* | **Chlamydia**<br>First identified in association with genital infection. A rare disease then, now common. |
| *1981* | **HIV** identified. Few cases then. Had killed over 100,000 Americans by the end of 1990. |
| *1984* | **Herpes** became common. Doctor office visits for treatment of herpes increased 15-fold between 1966–1984. |
| *1985–1990* | **HPV** (human papillomavirus) increased, especially in young people. Example: recent survey revealed 46 percent of sexually active coeds at U.C. (Berkeley) are infected. It is the cause of most cancer of the vulva, vagina, cervix, and penis. Death rate from HPV is about 4800 women annually—more women than are killed by AIDS. |
| *1990* | **Syphilis** is at a 40-year high.<br>**Pelvic inflammatory disease (PID)** infects 1 million American women. 16,000 to 20,000 teenagers infected.<br>Antibiotic resistant strains of **gonorrhea** present in all 50 states. |

*Then: before the sexual revolution of 1960–1990.
**Now: the result of that sexual revolution.**

# Scared About Sex?

"I'M SO SCARED!"

"I worry about that a lot."

"I'm feeling paranoid."

In the quiet of my office I sense and hear and can almost touch the fear that restlessly lives in so many women's hearts as they pour out to me their innermost thoughts about sex. I am their gynecologist. They know I am genuinely concerned about them as people, not just about their medical problems. So they share with me the worries that trouble their minds and hearts and have the potential to devastate their futures.

They know our conversation is private. What they say, what they are worried about, what they share and ask, will not be repeated to anyone. In this environment, women relax and often open up their hearts in a way they cannot do anywhere else. They are free to verbalize those feelings they may have been unable to express previously.

This is strikingly evident as I hear women, especially single women, agonize about their fears and concerns in the sexual area. From them I learn an enormous amount about very personal and sensitive issues. Without betraying any confidences, I want to share with you some of that knowledge in the hope it may benefit you.

Allow the experiences others have had to be a guide in your life. The sexual arena can be either a vicious jungle or a beautiful garden. The paths others have taken can help you establish a reliable road map for your journey through the tangle of life. Learning from others' experiences can bring you to that garden of fulfillment and peace.

What has caused something as wonderful as sexuality to become such a frightening issue to a large percentage of single women in our country? Isn't sex supposed to come as close to the unspoiled "Garden of Eden" intent as any of life's experiences?

Sex frightens many people (both men and women) because they know about horrible experiences friends have

---

### STD in 1991

*1 in 5 Americans is now infected with STD.*
*12 million people annually are new victims of STD.*
*35–50 different kinds of STD now exist.*

---

had with sexually transmitted disease. Some women are legitimately concerned about sex because of the way they or some of their friends have been treated by men who wanted only intercourse rather than a truly intimate, loving, caring relationship. Many read the headlines about the epidemic of sexually transmitted diseases racing through our society and are scared to death.

What do such headlines proclaim that so frightens them? One example is this quote from an information booklet published by the American College of Obstetricians and Gynecologists: "Except for the common cold and flu, sexually transmitted diseases are the most common diseases in the United States."

Another example is from *The Public Health Report* from the Centers for Disease Control (May-June 1985, vol. 100) where Parra and Cates, who are with the Division of Sexually Transmitted Disease, state, "The problem of sexually transmitted diseases (STDs) in the United States has been growing, in both scope and complexity, at an alarming rate."

In the *Journal of the American Medical Association* (Oct. 22/29, 1982, Volume 248) Edward N. Brandt, Jr., M.D. (Department of Health and Human Services, Washington, D.C.), stated, "The human tragedy [of STD] is terrible, and the conservatively estimated two billion dollars cost to all of us is an enormous burden."

In 1985 Roy Rivenburg, a freelance writer, made these comments:

> STDs have touched the lives of everyone from innocent spouses to a celibate nun, resulting in birth defects, cancer, sterility, and death among men, women, and even children, who never knew they had a disease. And the problem is expected to escalate to incredible proportions. Some experts predict that as many as one in four Americans of reproductive age will contract a sexually transmitted disease in his or her lifetime.

---

### STD in 1992

*1 in 4 Americans will be infected with STD.*

---

And in an article by V. C. Wright in *The Medical Aspects of Human Sexuality* (March 1989, 23:135), we read that "the younger a woman is when she begins sexual activity and the more sexual partners she has, the more likely she is to develop pre-cancerous changes in the cervix and actual cervical cancer."

In *The Journal of the American Medical Association* (June 23/30, 1989), we learn from a symposium in New York City on sexually transmitted diseases:

Authorities who have worked on stopping STD spread for years said "that the situation is now nearly out of control. With the permanent scarring that occurs in sexual organs from these diseases and without a reversal in this trend—we are going to have an entire infertile cohort (or an entirely infertile group of people in our society)."

Finally, women are legitimately frightened when they read about a specific individual, such as the one described in *The New England Journal of Medicine* (321:21, Nov. 23, 1989, pp. 1460-62):

> Detailing a mini-epidemic of AIDS started by one man, a Belgian researcher declared that women are at high risk of getting the disease. He told of a heterosexual consulting engineer from Rawanda in Central Africa who was living in Belgium and traveling between the two countries. After the engineer was diagnosed with AIDS in 1985, nineteen of his sexual contacts were traced, and seventeen of them agreed to be tested. Ten were found to be infected, Dr. Clumeck of St. Pierre Hospital in Brussels, told participants here at the International Conference on AIDS in Children, Adolescents, and Heterosexual Adults.
>
> Described as "handsome and highly sociable," the late engineer—who was not an intravenous drug user—spread the disease among a group of primarily professional women. He had about twenty to thirty sexual contacts per year before he became ill.
>
> Dr. Clumeck maintained that women are at greater risk than men for human immunodeficiency virus transfer and that a previous or concurrent sexually transmitted disease increases that risk.
>
> He pointed out that of the ten seropositive Belgian women, two had intercourse with the engineer only once.

Has this recent bombardment of frightening information affected your sexual attitudes and behavior? I hope so. If you are involved with a group of people whose lifestyle includes changing sexual partners, hasn't this question crossed your mind: "What if one of these men is promiscuous, or is bisexual and has AIDS?" I have one patient, an actress, who has experienced exactly this scenario. She has already seen a couple of friends die from AIDS and knows others suffering with the disease. She said to me, "I really worry that one of the men I am with will not be honest with me about being bisexual and that one of them might have AIDS." She said it is a "very, very scary situation." Sometime later she came back to report that she had decided to be celibate for the time being.

What if you are in your forties, widowed or divorced for two or three years, and dating occasionally? If you consider having intercourse with one of these men, do you worry about the possibility of contracting STD? Do you wonder what their past sexual experience might have been—what the possibilities are that they might have a sexually transmitted disease. Yet, you are so lonely for intimacy that those concerns seem inconsequential and get only momentary consideration. I understand the need for intimacy and closeness and will discuss these issues later.

If you are a teenage girl and have chosen not to have intercourse until you are married, have you worried about ever finding a husband who has not had prior sex? Do you wonder how you can be absolutely sure that the one you marry does not have a sexually transmitted disease when you marry him?

I recently met one young woman who is worried by that thought. As part of the sex education course at our local public high school, I handle the classes on the subject of sexually transmitted disease. Once as I talked about the tremendous danger of contracting sexually transmitted disease for people who have sex outside of marriage, I noticed a beautiful ninth-grade girl frown more and more. When we came to question time she slowly raised her hand, and with a very troubled countenance, said, "But even though I wait until I get married to have sex, won't all the guys out there have already had intercourse and therefore have these diseases?" I will discuss answers to her question later in this book, but I want to emphasize here the significance of a fifteen-year-old girl having to worry about whether or not her future husband would have a sexually transmitted disease when she married him. This is a sad commentary on the condition of our society!

Is all this terrible fear justified?

Good question. You may think that the news media is just doing their usual "exaggeration for the sake of sensationalism" thing. You may have a number of unmarried friends who are sexually involved, and—as far as you know—none has experienced the trauma of sexually transmitted disease.

This is one subject, however, about which the media is not "sensational" enough. These diseases are pervasive. They will cause people to slip off to the doctor without mentioning it to their closest friends. Sexually transmitted infections are embarrassing. I know, because I see those people when they quietly and fearfully appear in my office. My colleagues and I see these diseases in our offices all the time, and we know that the rates are rapidly increasing.

Remember, people with a sexually transmitted disease are not usually going to proclaim that fact to their friends. It may seem to you that no one you know has an STD, when the truth is that people all around us are infected right now. Often they themselves don't know it. If you (or your partner) have been having sex outside a marriage relationship, *you might be infected already.* Why do I make such a frightening statement? Well, first look back at the statements I quoted earlier in this chapter. They are true! Second, look at the following statistics.

1. *Herpes*—At least 30 percent of single sexually active Americans have been infected with this virus and can give it to their partners. Recent studies (see p. 118) give higher infection rates.

2. *Venereal Wart Virus*—About 30 percent of single sexually active Americans carry this virus. This is HPV, the human papillomavirus, and it causes venereal warts, precancerous changes and/or cancer to a woman's vulva,

vagina, and cervix. It also causes cancer of the penis in men.

3. *Chlamydia*—As many as 40 percent of specific groups of people in our country have this STD. The high incidence of chlamydia in teenagers and college students is alarming. Chlamydia infections often result in sterility in women. This infection is considered by many experts to be the most common STD in America.

4. *Gonorrhea*—The number of people in our society who have this infection is increasing at an alarming rate. As with chlamydia, the infectious agent causes pelvic inflammatory disease (PID), the second most common cause of hospital admission for women during the reproductive age of life (second only to childbirth). There is a great chance of sterility from PID, whether caused by gonorrhea or by chlamydia.

5. *Syphilis*—About 16 out of every 100,000 Americans have syphilis. This represents the highest rate of syphilis in our society since 1950. The rate increased 25 percent from 1986 to 1987 alone, the largest single year increase in thirty years. This trend continues today.

These statistics document how these diseases are spreading like a firestorm in our country. This rapid spread has been so pervasive that statistics verify the statements below, startling as they may be. If you can make yourself accept them as facts, and if you use this information wisely, you can avoid diseases that might otherwise ravage your life.

*Statement 1: A high percentage of unmarried men who have ever had intercourse with another partner will have a sexually transmitted disease they can pass on to you if you have sex with them.* Obviously, if a man has had intercourse with only one other woman and she never had intercourse with anyone else, he would not have STD. Statistics, however, show that 8 percent of single men have had five or more sex partners in the past year (reported from Centers for Disease Control). Correlated with that was a study done by Susan D. Cochran of California State University, North-

ridge, in which she found that 47 percent of the male subjects said they had told dates they had had fewer sexual
partners than they actually did. Approximately 23 percent
of the men said they would not tell a partner if they were
currently involved with someone else.

*Statement 2: When you are having sex with a person, you are
having sex with all the people he or she has ever had sex with, so
far as sexually transmitted disease is concerned.* There are
some obvious exceptions to this. For instance, if a man
were found to have been infected with chlamydia by a
previous partner but he had that infection cured with
antibiotics, you would not be exposed to that *particular*
infectious agent if you had sex with him. But if a man has
had sex with five women in the past and each of them had
had sex with five other men, and each of them had had sex
with five . . . , do you see how you can be exposed to STD
from innumerable people, some of whom may have had
dangerous sexual practices, such as group sex? Remember
that there is no known cure for any viral STD, including
herpes, HPV, AIDS, and hepatitis.

*Statement 3: Without medical data, you cannot know if some-
one with whom you are having intercourse or someone with
whom you plan to have intercourse has a sexually transmitted
disease.* Even if a man is honest when he tells you he has no
symptoms of STD, he may still be carrying infectious
agents of one of these diseases and can pass such a disease
to you. Many of these diseases can be present in a person's
body and produce absolutely no signs of infection, yet be
transmitted during intercourse.

For example, a study reported by M. H. Jadzek, M.D., in
*Canadian Family Physician* (Oct. 1985, 31:1861), showed that
over 75 percent of both men and women infected with
chlamydia had no symptoms of the infection. Yvonne
Bryson, M.D., Associate Professor of Pediatrics at the
University of California, Los Angeles School of Medicine,
was quoted in *American Medical Association News* (June 2,
1989), as saying that "there is a growing spread of an asymp-

tomatic herpes virus-type infection. This is a silent infection—you can get it from someone who has no symptoms. Without symptoms—even minor ones of burning or itching—transmission by those who are infected but unaware of it can become a dangerous cycle."

In the same *AMA News,* the Centers for Disease Control reported in 1989 that they have found 2 out of every 1,000 college students infected with the AIDS virus—almost all of these students were totally unaware that they were infected. So their sex partners were also unaware. Common sense would say, too, that many of these AIDS-infected students are the most likely to be sexually active and have many different sexual partners. If you are a college student, how would you know that a guy with whom you planned to have sex was not in the AIDS infected group, especially since he would probably not know it?

Are all these statements and facts and figures supposed to be scary? You bet they are! These problems are real. The damaging effects of STD can be mild but extremely aggravating, or they can be severe and permanent—as in death. Although these facts should alert you to the dangers, they shouldn't cause you to become a fearful person. Justifiable fear is extremely important and can protect you from harm. Fear of fire prevents people from being burned—that is "healthy" fear. But being so afraid of fire that you become neurotic and cannot bring yourself to ever be around any fire is unreasonable. It is wise to have enough fear of STD to make you pause and think about your sexual behavior. Letting your fear of STD make you afraid of marriage itself or of sex in marriage is unhealthy and unbalanced. As a matter of fact, one of my goals for this book is to help you have less fear of marital sex by enabling you and your present or future husband to have less chance of acquiring STD.

I have often heard it said that physicians can never scare people enough about sexually transmitted disease to halt the spread of these diseases, that doctors cannot cause people to abstain from sex outside of marriage even by instilling the fear of contracting gonorrhea, syphilis, or AIDS. I have even said that myself, many times. But I was absolutely wrong!

That might have been true when gonorrhea and syphilis were about the only STDs we had to deal with. But it seems that every few years human beings are assaulted (literally battered) with new sexually transmitted diseases. Each succeeding disease seems worse than the last. Herpes began terrorizing people in 1976. Chlamydia infections began making headlines in the early 1980s and is now one of the most prevalent STDs. The HPV virus that causes venereal warts and cancer of the cervix, vulva, vagina, and penis is now spreading faster than either herpes or chlamydia. Finally, the vicious plague of AIDS is seen as the monster it really is, arising like a giant demon from its obscurity a mere decade ago.

Yes, I have changed my mind about the fear quotient of STD. I think that knowing the facts can scare us into practicing sane and genuinely "safe" sex. It can also cause us to pause long enough to evaluate the proper role that sex should have in our lives. It can keep us from blindly following our emotions and falling unthinkingly, head over heels, into sexual liasons, only to end up invalids from such encounters.

Fact-based fear *should* operate in our lives, and we should let it help us in the sexual area. An example of how fear affects what we do is the way we obey the speed limit when we think a radar trap is up ahead of us on the highway. All it takes is for two approaching motorists to flash their lights in warning, and we slow down. Because we are reminded that we might have to pay a speeding ticket, we obey the law. Fear changes what we might otherwise do. And that is good. We should let fear of STD affect what we do sexually. Use the experiences of the patients documented here as warnings. See the information as blinking yellow lights that cause you to slow down and obey the rules of nature about sex.

Knowing that many single, sexually active people have an STD, you should be as afraid of having sex with one of them as you are of that officer with that radar gun. At the traffic court the penalty is only in dollars. In the sexual arena you could pay with your physical and emotional health, with a lot of money, with your integrity, and even with your life.

# 2

# Facts and Figures About STD

*What is sexually transmitted disease?*
*How would I know if I (or someone else) had one?*
*What is so special, so different about STD?*

Simply stated, a sexually transmitted disease (STD) is an infectious condition that is passed from one person to another during sexual activity. You may be more familiar with the term *venereal disease* (VD), a name more commonly used a few years ago.

During intimate sexual contact, body fluids and secretions are exchanged between partners. This exchange occurs not only during vaginal intercourse, but during other physical activity, including seemingly harmless "deep" kissing.

Since body secretions are not normally exchanged when people hug or shake hands, and since most STD germs cannot live long outside the human body, STDs are usually passed only during sexual activity. For that, the human race should be very grateful.

The most common sexual activity, and therefore the most common way to contract STD, is vaginal intercourse. Secretions of the vagina and penis are the most usual means of transmission of STD organisms. If a woman is infected with an STD, her vaginal secretions and often her vulva and vaginal tissues will contain these infectious agents. If a man is infected, his semen and often the skin of his penis and scrotum will contain such material.

Many people do not understand how a man can contract an STD through vaginal intercourse, because a man is not a "receptacle" for fluid in the sense that a woman is. The truth is, however, that during intercourse, a man's penis acts like a miniature vacuum cleaner. It will suction minute amounts of secretions from the woman's vagina into his urethra (the tube in the penis through which urine and semen flow). If the woman has a sexually transmitted disease, the man actually draws up the causative organisms into his reproductive organs where they can initiate infection.

Most material introduced into a woman's vagina will be absorbed into her bloodstream quickly. In fact, we often administer medications to a woman through her vagina if she cannot take them by mouth. Fluids deposited in the vagina can pass up through the uterus and tubes and appear in the abdominal cavity (where the ovaries and intestines are located) within five minutes.

During sexual intercourse, a woman's vagina is a receptacle for the teaspoon of semen a man normally ejaculates. If a man has an STD, his ejaculate can be filled with infectious materials. Portions of this ejaculate are rapidly absorbed into a woman's bloodstream. Other portions are passed through the uterus and tubes into the abdomen. Is it any wonder that women become infected with STD?

Some types of infection merely require certain types of skin contact between two people. (These include herpes, venereal warts, and others to be mentioned later.)

Sexually transmitted disease is contracted primarily during intimate sexual contact. Infectious STD agents from a partner's genital area may be transmitted to the mouth. Anal sex can cause infection of the rectum. Many of these diseases can also be transmitted from mouth to mouth.

You will not get STD from using the same telephone or typewriter, or holding the same tools or shaking hands. You will not get STD from toilet seats or from infected waiters in restaurants (unless, of course, you have sex with them). In general, *people get a sexually transmitted disease by having sex with other people who have a sexually transmitted disease.*

Most STD germs are very fragile. They require warmth and moisture; when they become dry, they die quickly. They are also sensitive to temperature change, to sunlight, and to other environmental influences. Outside the body, they are very weak and short-lived.

Inside the body, however, STD germs are extremely potent and can cause tremendous damage. The AIDS virus is a good example. Outside the body, it is easily killed by alcohol, bleach, and other mild disinfectants. Inside the human body it is a powerful monster and is essentially 100 percent fatal.

> ## *80 percent of those infected with STD have absolutely no symptoms.*

## General Symptoms

Some of the symptoms of sexually transmitted disease mimic other diseases; some of them might be noticed by men, others by women. Let's take a closer look at symptoms that *might* be caused by sexually transmitted disease. Men usually have fewer symptoms of STD than women do. Because a man's sex organs are not as moist as a woman's, the STD germs do not proliferate as rapidly and therefore are less likely to present a problem for a man. For this reason, men often do not know they have an STD. Women often do not know they have an STD because their genital organs are internal and the infection can hide inside their bodies.

Some of the possible signs or symptoms of STD that a *man* might notice (or that you might notice about a man) include the following:

1. *Discharge from the penis.* Any fluid (pus, discharge, secretions) from a man's penis other than urine or sperm (ejaculate) is cause to see a doctor. This symptom almost always indicates sexually transmitted disease. Gonorrhea or chlamydia would usually be the cause.

2. *Burning with urination.* A burning sensation during urination often indicates a sexually transmitted disease. A doctor should be consulted because gonorrhea and even chlamydia can cause this.

3. *Growths in the genital area.* Any growth on the penis or scrotum or in the anal area may mean venereal warts or other sexually transmitted infections. (*Any* new growth *anywhere* on the body should be seen by a physician, although those in parts of the body other than the genitals are less likely to indicate a sexually transmitted infection.)

4. *Sores on the genitals.* Small, tender sores on the genitals may be herpes ulcers. If they are painless, firm, and thickened, they may indicate syphilis. Such sores must be promptly evaluated by a doctor.

Possible symptoms of sexually transmitted disease that *both men and women* might have could be:

1. *Skin rashes or sores.* Both syphilis and AIDS can produce skin sores or rashes, and scabies can cause a very irritating rash. Any body rash should be evaluated by a physician.

2. *Enlarged lymph nodes.* AIDS and syphilis can cause enlargement of the lymph nodes all over the body. Some of the more unusual STDs can cause enlarged lymph nodes of the groin. (See chapter 16.)

3. *Long-lasting infections.* Any infections of the skin, lungs, or other parts of the body that do not clear up quickly should be checked by a doctor. AIDS and some other STDs can cause such problems.

4. *Inflammation of a joint.* If inflammation, redness, and swelling are present in a joint (such as a knee or an elbow), a physician should be seen. Gonorrhea can cause such infections. If there is a possibility of sexually transmitted infection, this should be mentioned to the doctor.

5. *Yellow eyes, dark urine.* Signs of hepatitis include the whites of the eyes turning yellow or the urine turning Coca-Cola colored. Hepatitis B is one of the most common sexually transmitted diseases in the world.

6. *Itching of the pubic hair.* Pubic lice can cause such itching. (See chapter 16.)

Some of the symptoms of sexually transmitted disease in females include:

1. *Vaginal discharge.* Although a vaginal discharge does not always indicate sexually transmitted disease, it *always* should be evaluated. If the discharge could possibly be caused by sexual contact, that should be mentioned to a physician. Vaginal discharge can be a symptom of gonorrhea, chlamydia, herpes, or even of HPV (cause of venereal warts).

2. *Sores on the genitals.* Ulcers on the vulvar area, especially if urination causes discomfort, may indicate herpes. If a sore is slightly thickened and painless, it could be syphilis. Any sore or lump, especially if not tender, should be evaluated.

3. *Growths in the genital area.* Growths around the vulva, inside the vagina, or around the anus may be venereal warts. Treatment is most important, because the virus that causes these warts is the most common cause of cervical, vulvar, and vaginal cancer.

4. *Burning with urination.* Normally, a burning sensation with urination merely indicates a bladder infection. As the

urine pours out over herpes ulcers, however, the burning may be quite intense. Whether the burning is caused by herpes or by bladder infection, it should be diagnosed and treated by a doctor.

5. *Lower abdominal pain, especially with fever.* A woman with a gonorrhea or chlamydia infection may carry the germs for many months without symptoms. When either of these germs begins actively spreading in the body, pelvic inflammatory disease is usually the result, causing abdominal pain and fever. These symptoms should be checked by a doctor immediately. The sooner an infection of this type is treated, the less likely it is that sterility will result.

If you have symptoms that you think may be caused by sexually transmitted disease, see your doctor immediately. Tell him or her of your suspicions. You may be surprised to know that STDs are often difficult to diagnose in women, so you need to help your doctor in the search as much as you can. Remember, doctors are not mind readers. There is no way they will know you may have recently changed sex partners. Unless your doctor knows the details of your sexual activity, diagnosis may be hampered and delayed. Your doctor is there to help you. The information about your sex life is just between you, the doctor, and his or her staff. If you are an adult, the facts will go no further (unless you have a disease that is reportable to the health department).

So you can help your doctor be of more help to you. The more quickly you get that help, the better. The longer a sexually transmitted disease is active in your body, the more irreversible damage it can do. Time is a crucial factor. For instance, if you let a chlamydia infection burn in your body without treatment even a few days too long, it greatly increases your chance of being sterile—of never having a baby except possibly by in vitro fertilization or adoption.

Remember that your symptoms are not necessarily from a sexually transmitted disease. Many STD symptoms mirror symptoms of other diseases that may have nothing whatever to do with sexual activity. For instance, many women develop small bumps on their labia, called inclusion cysts. These are not dangerous and are definitely not a sexually transmitted disease. But venereal warts can feel almost exactly the same! A doctor can easily tell the difference. If you are concerned, you can be quickly reassured by seeing your physician.

A second reason that you should immediately see a doctor if you think you have a sign or symptom of an STD is that both women and men frequently have a second (or even third) sexually transmitted disease along with the first. The symptoms of the second disease may not yet be present. The best example of this is the fact that people who have gonorrhea will often also have chlamydia. It has recently been found that anyone who has an ulcer of the genitals is much more likely to become infected with AIDS—and the most common cause of ulcers of the genitals is other STDs (herpes or syphilis). Therefore, if you think you might have STD symptoms, please see a doctor and get all appropriate testing done. Doing this promptly could preserve your health and even save your life.

## The Side Effects

There is one misconception I want to clear up at this point. *Having had an STD does not provide immunity against that disease or against any other STD.* You can get them over and over again—every time you are intimate with a man carrying the infectious agents. Each time you are infected with a disease such as gonorrhea or chlamydia, you develop more and more scarring in your female organs and have an ever-increasing chance of sterility in the future.

We can use chlamydia as an example. One infection with chlamydia gives a woman a 25 percent chance of becoming sterile. A second infection results in a 50 percent chance of infertility. A third infection causes a 75 percent rate of infertility. Repeated gonorrhea infections do the same thing, but each of the chlamydia percentages is cut in half with gonorrhea. With both these diseases, not only can infertility result, but its female victims can suffer from persistent, year-after-year abdominal pain from the pelvic inflammatory disease caused by these infections. This PID pain can become so intolerable and/or dangerous that it can necessitate a hysterectomy. These infections can also damage a woman's fallopian tubes and greatly increase her chance of tubal pregnancies. Furthermore, every time she has a tubal pregnancy and must have it removed surgically, it lowers her chance of *ever* having a child. (See Part Two for detailed discussions of chlamydia and gonorrhea.)

The foregoing observations are not just theories. I have had to operate on many, many women for these reasons. When I began my practice, one of my first surgical patients was a woman I was called to see as a consultant. She had been in the hospital one week with temperatures reaching 103 degrees every day. She had a ruptured abscess from one of her ovaries. Since antibiotics were not effective, I had to remove the uterus, tubes, and ovaries of this young woman and she was sterile from then on.

I saw a new patient yesterday who last year had a pregnancy develop in one of her fallopian tubes because of scarring from a chlamydia or gonorrhea infection. By the time the tubal pregnancy was found, the tube had ruptured. She needed major surgery to remove the tube and save her life. Unfortunately, X-rays now show that her remaining tube became totally obstructed by her STD. She is now sterile, all because of these infections and their side effects.

## Who Else Should Know?

If you have one of these diseases, your doctor will not report you to the police. It is not against the law to have an STD. Your doctor wants to see you get well as quickly as possible so you will not experience the agony of "STD gone wild."

Some states do require a physician to report *certain* STDs to the local health departments. This stipulation has been misunderstood by many people. Some states have such laws for statistical purposes and to track down people who have STD, but the intent of the law is to find infected people quickly so they can be treated. Until they are treated, they are like a time bomb. Their disease is quietly ticking. Eventually it explodes—maiming and damaging and destroying, not just them but other people to whom they might have unwittingly passed the disease (or diseases).

## Special Words for Teens

Teenagers are far more likely to be infected with sexually transmitted diseases and to be damaged by those diseases than an adult is. The cervix of a teenage girl has a an outer covering (columnar epithelium) which is more susceptible to being infected by the bacteria and viruses of sexually transmitted disease. Teenagers also have lower levels of antibodies against infection in their bodies. Adults have been exposed to many types of germs and generally have a high level of antibodies. Teenagers do not have this broad protection and are, therefore, much more likely to be infected when exposed to germs.

Teenagers have some menstrual cycles which occur without ovulation. Actually, in the first two years after a girl begins having periods she will often have a period without ovulation. This causes the cervical mucus to be more fluid in consistency and, therefore, more permeable to germs, allowing her to be infected more easily.

If teenagers start having sex, they have more sexual partners. Apparently, when a teenager starts a lifestyle of sexual intercourse, he or she adopts a mentality of relating to the opposite sex by having intercourse—even when he or she leaves one partner and moves to another one. The Centers for Disease Control in its *Morbidity and Mortality Weekly Report* of January 4, 1991 (vol. 39: 51, 52), showed that if adolescents started having sex before the age of eighteen, at the time they were interviewed 70 percent of them had

had two or more sexual partners and 45 percent had had four or more sexual partners. This was compared with people who began having intercourse after the age of nineteen. Only 20 percent of these people had had two or more sexual partners, and only 1 percent had had four or more sexual partners. The more sexual partners a person has, the more likely he or she is to be infected by sexually transmitted disease. There is a strong correlation between the number of sexual partners and infection with these diseases.

If you are under eighteen years of age and have a sexually transmitted disease, and you do not want your parents to know about your infection, you pose a special problem for your physician. Every physician handles such patients differently and usually on an individual basis.

Generally, young women have difficulty totally understanding the terrible impact that damage from an STD can have on their futures. For instance, I find that very few of my under-eighteen patients react when I tell them that one chlamydia infection can give them a 25 percent chance of being sterile the rest of their lives. However, perhaps your mother has had a fertility problem in the past and knows the years of heartbreak and expense and agony that go with infertility. In that case, she better than anyone else, can get this across to you, her daughter. For this and many more reasons, I think your parents should know about your STD problems if you are a minor.

I will give one more reason I have this opinion: testing for STD is expensive. I have seen many young women who had been exposed to STD refuse testing because they did not have the money to pay for the tests. They felt they could not ask their parents to pay for these tests because then the parents would know they were sexually active. Instead, they allow the STD to continue to grow and produce its havoc, rather than confide in their parents and receive their help and counsel.

This is the kind of short-sightedness that can indeed be a problem for you as a teenager. Try to accept the fact that it doesn't matter *who* knows about your STD if it will result in your receiving prompt, effective treatment and thereby prevent catastrophic health problems for you in the future.

One of the most withering, ice-cold looks I have ever received came from a sixteen-year-old who was seeing me about the possibility of STD without her mother's knowledge—even though her mother was waiting in the reception room. When I suggested discussing her situation with her mother, she gave me that look as she said, "I don't believe it is any of her business." Because of this attitude, she did not want me to do tests for STD because her mother would be billed and would know the daughter was having sex. If I had followed this young woman's wishes, she would probably be sterile today. That is a terrible price to pay just to keep a mother in the dark. Parents are your best friends, although you may not always think so! They care more about you than anyone else in the world, so they can also help you more than anyone else. Accept their love and their help—you will be forever glad you did. There are always exceptions to any generalization, of course. If you honestly believe that your family situation is such that you simply cannot tell a parent about your disease, tell your doctor that, too. Perhaps he or she can give you an alternative that makes sense both medically and emotionally.

## Some Related Costs

The expense of testing mentioned above brings up the subject of cost. Most people who are having sex outside of marriage (or thinking about it) don't ever consider the dollar costs—until they go to the doctor to be tested. Testing for STD is expensive. If only one test were sufficient, the problem would not be so great. Remember, though, because of the possible coexistence of different STDs in one individual, when we suspect one disease we are often compelled to test for other diseases.

For example, yesterday I saw a twenty-six-year-old woman who had been in a five-year sexual relationship with one man. Soon after they broke up a few months ago, she began having sex with another man. When I asked, "Are you concerned about STD?" she said, "Yes" and asked to be tested. I had to tell her that the very least we could do to be safe would be to culture for chlamydia and gonorrhea and do blood tests for AIDS and syphilis. In our city the total cost for this is about $150. And this is not just a one-time expense. A chlamydia culture can be wrong as much as 15 percent of the time. It can take a year before an AIDS victim has a positive test result. Both tests could need repeating later. Also, anytime she or her sexual partner has sex with anyone else, the entire series of tests should be repeated. This is true for anyone who changes sexual partners.

Obviously, tremendous expense is involved just in testing, and this doesn't include the expense of treatment if infection is present. Remember that any individual's treatment expense is always doubled, because both partners must be treated at the same time to prevent Ping-Pong (continually going back and forth) infections.

All these initial costs do not represent the really expensive part of the total STD picture. The expense of hospitalization can be a huge hidden part of the financial iceberg. The most common cause of hospitalization of women in the reproductive age of life, except for childbirth, is pelvic inflammatory disease (PID), usually caused by gonorrhea and/or chlamydia. Billions of dollars are spent on treating such infections every year. Since this is the kind of infection that causes women to become sterile, later in life there may be the enormous expense of infertility evaluation and treatment, of laparoscopies, microsurgery, and in vitro fertilization (test-tube baby procedures) to help these women conceive. In all this we have not yet mentioned the expenses incurred by hundreds of thousands of AIDS sufferers. Some experts predict that the expense of treating people with AIDS will literally destroy the economics of the American health-care system as the costs grow into the multiple billions of dollars.

## Implications

In this chapter we have discussed the general nature of STD, including the symptoms of some of these diseases. (We will talk much more specifically and extensively about the individual diseases in the second part of this book.) The overview presented in this chapter can best help you to know what to watch for. Whether or not you are having intercourse, and whether or not you think you are having symptoms of STD, you need to see your doctor and have a Pap smear and pelvic and breast exam every year. The ultimate goal of a good physician is the same goal I hope you have for yourself—to prevent disease, not merely to treat it after it is established. I urge you, therefore, to see your physician for regular checkups and also to see him or her if you have any questions about your health, including how your lifestyle may be affecting it. This book is meant as a reference guide and an education tool. But do not diagnose yourself. Above all, never fail to seek medical help because you have convinced yourself that you may have a sexually transmitted disease (or any other disease, for that matter).

# 3

# When Is Sex "Safe"?

I WAS RECENTLY visiting with a friend who has a son in college. We were talking about modern-day sexual practices as related to sexually transmitted disease. He said, "Joe, my son will finish college, then probably go to graduate school before he gets married. I think it is unrealistic in this day and age to expect him not to have intercourse until then." Assumptions such as this underlie much of the sexual activity that has caused STD to spread through our society like a plague, until we now face the fact that many sexually active single people in our country are infected.

The thought seems to be "Since I cannot or do not want to get married now, and since I am not about to go without sex, I will have sex with whom I want, when I want. It really can't hurt me."

But suddenly we find that it *has* hurt many people already and is hurting many more every day. Women are the primary victims in the long run! Sexual activity can hurt in simple and small ways or in large, painful ways. I saw a patient last year with her first outbreak of herpes. The interesting thing was that this woman had last had intercourse two years before. Suddenly she discovered that she had a sexually transmitted disease as a legacy of a long-past affair.

I also remember the college girl from our town who went to school in another city. She developed a moderately abnormal Pap smear and was told by a doctor in that city that this was all due to "the stress of college classes." Of course it was not due to stress; it was due to an STD infection caused by the venereal wart virus caught from her boyfriend—the first and only person with whom she had ever had intercourse. This young woman had to undergo laser surgery and will be okay physically. But talk about stress! She had to come back home for treatment, discuss all this with her parents, have general anesthesia, and spend a lot of money to pay the bills. She could have avoided all this. So can you!

Many a father predicts that his son will inevitably have sex before marriage and excuses it as a "normal but a little naughty" process. The assumption here is that this kind of sex is a relatively innocuous affair, fun to participate in occasionally, harmless, a little immoral, but still okay. The truth is that when an unmarried person starts relating to a person of the opposite sex by having intercourse, that basis for relationships usually persists, even if the partners change. To put it bluntly, sex itself becomes a habit, a lifestyle. When that happens, the person will unconsciously gravitate only toward relationships that involve sexual intimacy.

I hope that after reading this book, gaining more understanding about STD, and thinking about your own life, you who are single and sexually active will see why it is wise to change. You who have not yet had sex will, I hope, realize that it is a lot easier to never have premarital intercourse than it is to change from a sexually active lifestyle to celibacy until marriage. The assumption that sex outside of marriage is "harmless fun" is dead wrong. It *is* a big deal and can have horrifying consequences for you and those you love.

## Pros and Cons of "Safe Sex" Techniques

The big question then, *if* all this can be avoided, is HOW? The surest protection against STD is abstaining from *any* premarital (and extramarital) sexual activity. Many people think that is "unrealistic" for them. The following remarks are directed at those who do not choose (or are tempted not to choose) abstinence. I think the way to start this discussion is to tell the opposite—how STD is *not* avoided. There are so many organizations, groups, societies, and people that are telling us how to have "safe sex" that it is hard to know what is true and what is not true. Who and what can you believe? This is an absolutely vital question for you because you are dealing with not only your future health and fertility, your future freedom from worry and financial difficulties, but also your future freedom from guilt and regret over what might have been.

> **The FDA allows condom manufacturers to market condoms that have three or fewer holes per 1000 condoms. Condoms rupture about 7 percent of the time during use.**

### Condoms

As I was watching TV a few months ago, a public-health advertisement came on the screen. It showed a sad-looking woman in obviously poor health whose message concerned the danger of sex without condoms. "Protect yourself from sexually transmitted disease by using condoms," she said. "If you will do this and have *safe sex,* you won't get AIDS, like I did." I found myself suddenly flushed with anger. I was so surprised at that anger that I forced myself to evaluate my reaction. I decided that there were two major facts about that ad that bothered me.

First, the advertisement implied that using condoms will absolutely prevent sexually transmitted infection. Impressionable young people—and older people looking for new answers—may be duped by such ads into believing that condoms will provide them with guaranteed safe sex. This is simply not true.

Think about it. There is a 10 to 25 percent chance of pregnancy every year in women who are depending on condoms for contraception. We forget or ignore the fact that although the egg lives only twenty-four hours, sperm can live and be fertile for two to three days. If a woman has intercourse two or three days before her egg is released, she can become pregnant.

If condoms cannot always prevent pregnancy, which can only occur (normally) during one twenty-four-hour period of time each month, they certainly will not prevent STD, which can be transmitted twenty-four hours a day, every day of the year. And germs are a lot smaller than sperm.

---

**Condoms often do not prevent sexually transmitted disease. Each year 25 percent of women whose partners use condoms for contraception get pregnant.**

---

Why do condoms fail? The primary reason is discipline. For condoms to have a chance of working to prevent STD, they must be used without fail during every single act of intercourse. This means that if my friend's college-age son started having sex when he was nineteen and did not get married until he was twenty-eight, he would have to use condoms *every* time he had intercourse during those nine years. Even married couples who use condoms for contraception are not that disciplined, and they have the practical advantages of not being rushed; being in the same bed most of the time; having a bedside table in which to keep the condoms; a relative degree of maturity; and the strong desire to avoid pregnancy. Yet, those people who produce the TV ads about using condoms to prevent disease seem to feel that all teenaged couples, or even older singles, can have the discipline and the condoms needed to maximize the safety factor. This is almost an impossibility, and it is one reason why sexually transmitted disease is running rampant among single sexually active people despite the media hype about condoms.

Here is another startling fact about condoms. From 10 to 20 percent of them have manufacturing defects. *Parade* magazine's "Special Intelligence Report" of January 1989, reported that condoms are not 100 percent protective: "Recent tests have shown that 12 percent of condoms made abroad failed." They further stated, "Unfortunately, there is *virtually no scientific* data on the failure rate of condoms." Some tests on condoms show a 10 to 20 percent failure rate when tested by filling them with water. It is very likely that condoms fail much more often than this under the stress of intercourse.

Then there is a third issue about condoms: They must be used correctly. They deteriorate if they are not stored in a cool, dry place. They must be handled with care to avoid damage and must be put on and removed properly. The media and public health officials are asking you who are having sex outside of marriage to always do all of these things, year after year, without exception.

Recently a group of sex educators was asked a question by a lecturer: "Imagine that you were approached by the man or woman of your dreams, the person you thought would be the best sex partner for you in all the world. If this person offered himself or herself to you but said, 'I want you to know that I have AIDS,' *would you have sex with that person, using only a condom for protection?*" In this sophisticated audience of educators, no one raised a hand at first. Finally one person slowly raised his hand. Then the lecturer asked the group, "Why, if *you* are unwilling to trust condoms, are you encouraging students throughout the country to rely on them for protection against AIDS and many other diseases?"

In the midst of all this discussion, you may forget the fact that the man with whom you are having intercourse may have an AIDS virus. That virus is lying quietly in his genital organs, coiled to strike like a rattlesnake. It literally will kill you if you fail to follow every one of the instructions about condom use. Even then, because of defects in manufacture, you still have a chance of being infected by the AIDS virus. Remember the "handsome, highly sociable man" described in the first chapter? He spread AIDS among a group of primarily professional women, although two of the women he infected had intercourse with him only one time each. If the "one time" your condoms fail you is when you are having sex with a man who has AIDS, there is a great chance that your life (as you now know it) will soon be over because of your being infected with that disease.

I personally feel that the "safe sex" and all the sex education and government-endorsed guidelines about condoms are just setting a booby trap for you. Instead of telling you that you will be protected if you use condoms, they should mention that if you are sexually active, you have a 20 percent chance per year of becoming pregnant and almost a 100 percent chance over a period of years of becoming pregnant and/or developing an STD infection *even if you use condoms.*

The inescapable fact is that, during one act of intercourse, condoms *may* protect against STD, but for frequent, repeated acts of intercourse over a period of months and years, *they will not.* The only way that there is any real safety from STD or pregnancy with condoms is for a couple to use two mechanical barriers. For example, the man must use a condom and the woman must use a contraceptive foam, or the woman can use both a diaphragm and its jelly and just before intercourse insert some contraceptive foam. However, you must use both of them every single time you have intercourse for them to have a reasonable chance of being effective against STD. Even then, you have no guarantee. Studies have shown that contraceptive foam does not always kill STD germs. Remember, too, that if a portion of his skin that is infected with herpes, crabs, or

HPV, touches your skin, you can get these infections even though you were using mechanical barriers for the act of intercourse.

With or without instructions as to their proper use, intensive sex education and condom ads have apparently not significantly increased the use of condoms. *The American Journal of Public Health* published a report (April 1989) showing that among sexually active girls in San Francisco (average age, 16.7 years), condom use *fell* from 27 to 23 percent in one year. The article commented, "Among homosexual men, condom use is equally infrequent. The National Institute of Health found that *two-thirds* of those engaging in anal intercourse do not use condoms."

Perhaps all those people who are not using condoms realized that they were fooling themselves if they depended on condoms for protection from STD! Maybe they decided to cut out the bother and enjoy sex without those impediments, relying just on chance that they would not get a sexually transmitted disease. I don't recommend this, of course, but the facts show that neither the condoms nor the education programs about them are working.

### Oral Contraceptives

As for the possible role of birth-control pills (oral contraceptives) in the prevention of STD, many studies have shown that if a woman uses oral contraceptives, she has less chance of being infected by gonorrhea than if she does not. I believe these studies are true, but they are true only of gonorrhea. A woman is not protected from chlamydia, HPV, herpes, or any of the other STDs just because she is using an oral contraceptive. And remember that chlamydia is far more prevalent and usually a far worse infection than gonorrhea.

### IUDs

Intrauterine devices (IUDs) offer no protection against sexually transmitted disease. As a matter of fact, if a woman is using an IUD, she is more likely to get PID (pelvic inflammatory disease) than a woman who is not using one. For this reason I do not think any woman should have an IUD inserted until she has had all the children she ever wants to have. Then, if she is unfortunate enough to develop a pelvic infection and become sterile, she will not also have to agonize over the children she can no longer bear.

### Can Medicine Keep You Well?

You may be agreeing with me that condoms do not make sex absolutely safe, even if used with contraceptive foam. You may understand that the "pill" and IUDs offer essentially no protection against STDs. If you are like many people, however, you may be saying, "I agree with you on that point, but of course you must be wrong when you conclude that the only way to have "safe" sex is in a monogamous marriage relationship." You may be thinking that even if you get a sexually transmitted disease, all you have to do is go to the doctor or a clinic and get it treated. With that attitude, you are really saying that you are expecting your doctor or clinic and modern science to provide a great big safety net.

Let me show you how that direction in your thinking can cause you to fall from your sexual trapeze and through huge gaping holes in the safety net of science. The result will be physical damage to your body that can cause you a lifetime of pain and suffering. Medical science does not have all the answers, especially in the realm of sexually transmitted disease.

A recent pharmaceutical advertisement that crossed my desk stated: "Living in the city is lonely enough. With herpes it is like solitary confinement." The ad continued, "Prevent genital herpes recurrences month after month with daily therapy." It showed a happy, smiling girl with three smiling friends. Such advertisements imply that medicine has finally triumphed over herpes—but that is far from the case. Herpes is a viral infection and has no known cure. It is still a major physical and emotional problem to most of those people who have it, even though it rarely constitutes any danger.

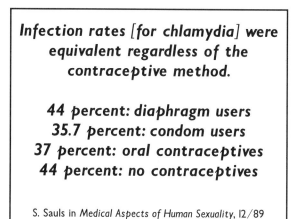

*Infection rates [for chlamydia] were equivalent regardless of the contraceptive method.*

***44 percent: diaphragm users***
***35.7 percent: condom users***
***37 percent: oral contraceptives***
***44 percent: no contraceptives***

S. Sauls in *Medical Aspects of Human Sexuality*, 12/89

Most people today assume that antibiotics can take care of chlamydia and gonorrhea and that syphilis is no longer a problem because it is responsive to penicillin. They believe that the majority of sexually transmitted diseases are curable and that even AIDS will succumb to the miracles of modern medicine someday soon. Continued references in newspapers and magazines picture the relentless effort on the part of researchers to find vaccines and cures for all of these diseases.

A patient whom I treated intermittently during the past few years would probably be a little angry if someone tried to reassure her about the triumph of science over HPV. Although she is well now, she has just completed a course of treatment for venereal warts that has spanned almost four years of her life and has cost about four thousand dollars. Her nightmare has included recurrent, aggravating warts; abnormal Pap smears, indicating precancerous changes in her cervix and vulva; numerous medications; and cervical and vulvar laser treatment.

There are several reasons why medicine has not yet solved (and may never solve) the STD problem for you or for anyone else:

1. *Many STDs are viral infections, and no human disease caused by a virus has a cure.* Herpes, HPV, AIDS, and hepatitis B are all caused by viruses. Some of these diseases can get better with time or can be somewhat helped by medication, but they have no cure. When you are infected with one of these viruses, your body may bear that infection for the rest of your life. An example would be hepatitis B, which is one of the world's most common STDs. About 10 percent of people who are infected with this disease become chronically ill and can develop cirrhosis of the liver or liver cancer or can become lifetime carriers of hepatitis B.

2. *Medical treatment may help your body get rid of the infectious organisms, but by the time that is accomplished much damage may have been done to your body.* This is common with gonorrhea and chlamydia. Even one infection with either one of these diseases can produce extensive scarring in the female organs and cause lifetime sterility. Then the only hope of becoming pregnant may be through very expensive infertility surgery or with in vitro fertilization (test-tube-baby procedures).

3. *The cost of treating STD is very high* and, at times, enormous. Another example is that because of the resistance of the gonorrhea germ, this infection must often now be treated with antibiotics that cost ten times as much as penicillin.

4. *Many STD organisms do not respond easily to treatment and are becoming resistant to antibiotics and medications.* Gonorrhea is the clearest example of such resistance, but there are reports in our medical literature of the resistance to treatment that other organisms have acquired. Chlamydia, the most common STD in America, is another example. An article by Shepard and Jones in *Fertility and Sterility*, Vol. 52, No. 2, August 1989, stated, "Chronic active chlamydial infection is frequently associated with tubal infertility [women being unable to get pregnant due

to damaged fallopian tubes], and may persist despite therapy." Already there are some reports that some AIDS viruses are developing resistance to AZT, the only good drug for that disease.

5. *Human nature being what it is, a perfect medical cure will never be the total solution for AIDS or any other STD.* You may find this a startling statement, and at first you may disagree with me. Why am I so pessimistic? We have had the perfect scientific cure for syphilis since penicillin was discovered, and it has not eradicated syphilis. (The incidence of syphilis in the USA is now at a forty-year high.)

Medical science cannot help people unless it can find them and treat them. Finding victims is difficult because up to 80 percent of all STDs produce no symptoms at first so that many infected people do not even know they have these diseases.

The next problem is getting people to go to a doctor if they think they might have an infection. Few of us like going to the doctor and admitting we are ill. People who think they might have an STD are usually even less willing to be diagnosed, due to the somewhat "embarrassing" nature of the way the disease was contracted. When I see a patient with an STD I always tell her to have her partner see a doctor. Many, many times these women return and tell me that their friend will not go. Often, the only persuasive technique these women have found effective is to refuse to have intercourse with these men until they have been examined and treated. It would be much better in the first place if they would not have sex with their partners until they were married. Then there would not only be "love" but also unconditional moral, legal, verbal, and physical commitment between two people. Within a faithful marriage, a closed sexual circle is formed, and neither mate needs to worry about STD as long as that bond is unbroken (assuming that neither of the parties was infected when the marriage began).

## These Facts Don't Lie

If you are trusting in medical science to bail you out if you should contract an STD, perhaps you need to be aware of the following facts:

1. *Syphilis.* Although this disease is relatively easy to treat (one shot of penicillin will usually suffice), diagnosing it is difficult. From the moment this dangerous disease is contracted, the germ is present, but you can be totally unaware that you are carrying it. Most women do not know they have syphilis until they have a blood test. Just as undetected termites can damage a building, so undetected syphilis can do devastating hidden damage to a human body.

2. *Gonorrhea.* In the past, the gonorrhea organism was simple to find and treat. A culture grown from vaginal or penile secretions could determine its presence, and a penicillin injection would take care of the problem. But some gonoccal bacteria have developed a resistance to penicillin, and this "resistant" strain is now present in every state in the United States.

The cost to treat this type of gonorrhea is more than ten times what it was in the past, and the number of its victims is increasing dramatically. The major problem, though, is not the dollar cost of treatment, but the potential human cost of the disease. Before gonorrhea is detected in a woman, she may already have become permanently sterile from fallopian tube damage. Also, many women have had to have hysterectomies because of gonorrhea infections.

3. *Herpes.* Although Zovirax (acyclovir) can make herpes symptoms more tolerable, it does not cure the disease. Once herpes is contracted, more than 50 percent of infected men or women will continue to have future outbreaks. One patient of mine has herpes lesions on her vulva with every menstrual period. Many women experience outbreaks not only with menstrual periods, but with every act of intercourse!

4. *HPV.* The venereal warts virus causes cancerous changes to a woman's vulva, vagina, and cervix. It also

causes cancer of the penis. While it is true that a yearly Pap smear will normally catch early HPV damage before it turns into cancer, HPV still necessitates frequent visits to the doctor's office for further exams, biopsies, and treatment. One of my patients was treated ten years ago for precancerous changes on her cervix and was back in my office this week because of an abnormal Pap smear. She will have to undergo more cervical surgery all because of a sexually transmitted disease.

5. *Chlamydia*. This disease can be treated with tetracycline, but it must be detected before it can be treated—and 70 percent of those who have chlamydia don't know it! Even when chlamydia is diagnosed and treated, scarring may have already caused sterility that will continue to haunt a woman for years.

6. *AIDS*. This disease is a thousand times more elusive and difficult to deal with than gonorrhea or syphilis. There may never be a cure for AIDS, and most authorities feel a vaccine to prevent it is years away. The majority of AIDS victims are initially unaware that they have become infected. Though AZT helps some AIDS patients live longer if they receive it early in their disease, it is not a cure. Currently, science does not have the answer for AIDS.

Researchers will continue to work on treatment and cures for STDs, and rightfully so, but it is important to know that you cannot depend on medical science to be a safety net for your sexual behavior.

## Understanding Your Doctor

Don't expect to hear all this information from your doctor or your health clinic. Some medical professionals simply do not have the time to discuss anything but the basics of your case. If you are concerned about STD, use this book to help you know which questions to ask your doctor about your individual situation. He or she is the one who will be in charge of testing and treating you. Your doctor may not necessarily *initiate* a discussion about STD, even if you have an infection. Also, your doctor may not discuss STD *in depth* with you. There are a number of reasons for this, some of which may be:

*Doctors like to cure people.* They are frustrated about being unable to cure a viral disease. For instance, they may therefore talk about being able to *treat* herpes with Zovirax but not discuss the fact that Zovirax *does not cure herpes* (and that herpes will come back when Zovirax is stopped). Be sure that you know what to expect in the future from any STD you might already have.

*Doctors don't like to appear to be moralizing.* Last month I talked to a medical student who had recently made rounds with his professor. One patient they saw was a young woman who had a sexually transmitted infection that was causing PID. The student asked the professor later if they shouldn't warn the woman of the possibility of future infertility if she continued her present sexual habits. The professor said, "Oh, no! We can't say something like that to her because that is a *moral* issue."

This student felt bad for the young woman because he knew that if she did not change her lifestyle, she would become infected again and then the possibility of her becoming infertile would increase dramatically. I don't consider it "moralizing" to tell a woman how she can avoid sexually transmitted disease, but some doctors do.

*Doctors become burned out by telling patients to do things for their health's sake and then having patients not do them.* All physicians get the feeling at one time or another that they are wasting their time telling patients how they can avoid disease. If they tell patients to stop smoking, many ignore the advice. When physicians tell them to exercise so they will be healthier, patients sometimes reject that idea, too. Is it any wonder that a physician believes that telling a woman to stop having sex outside of marriage so she will be healthier will not change anything in her behavior?

I believe that doctors should be telling their patients more about STD. I think it is worthwhile even if only a few people listen to the facts and change. That is why I am writing this book. Many of you who read it will not change, though. I wish you would. Some of you will hear this warning message and will avoid sex until marriage.

I think it is important for physicians to take the time to warn their patients. Physicians most likely will be forced in the future to tell patients more about STD, because STD is becoming more and more an epidemic. The information physicians provide must underscore what *OB/GYN News*, a national newsletter for obstetricians and gynecologists, stated in 1988: "Abstinence or sexual intercourse with a mutually faithful, uninfected partner are the most effective ways to reduce the risk of sexually transmitted disease infection." So, although today your doctor may not advise you about changing your sexual activity or may not discuss some of the other information included in this book, as time goes by, I think he or she will do so.

## How Sex Education Falls Short

Not only may your doctor omit some of the facts about STD, but also you may not have received important information from school sex-education programs. There are many reasons why such programs fail to emphasize certain information. The primary reason most sex-education teachers avoid being straightforward is that they don't believe people will change. In effect, they are assuming the worst about their students. I am offended by that attitude and hope you are, too.

Many people will choose a healthier lifestyle if they just have the facts. Sex-education teachers will emphasize using condoms, but you have just read in this chapter that condoms cannot guarantee "safe" sex. Sex educators tell me that they teach about condoms because single people will have sex anyway, and at least condoms provide *some* protection. "Some protection" would not be enough for me—not with the deadly specter of AIDS lurking around. If the people teaching about sexuality are not emphasizing the high failure rate of condoms, they are not being honest.

The main goal of some sex-education teachers may be to help people avoid pregnancy. Since conception can normally occur only during one twenty-four-hour period each month, condoms are fairly effective in spacing pregnancy for married couples. They are not totally effective in preventing pregnancy. *But if you are a single woman and you do get pregnant, it is usually a tragedy financially and emotionally. However, it is not nearly so much a problem for you as contracting a sexually transmitted disease that can literally ruin the rest of your life.* Although a pregnancy may sometimes be "a heartache," it is at least a normal condition for the female body.

Sexually transmitted disease is an enemy, a destroyer of the human body. I believe you should commit to follow any ideas that will protect you from STD; fortunately, the same measures that will protect against STD will also prevent an unwanted pregnancy. I will explain in chapter 5 the only reliable method to accomplish this. Let me repeat here that oral contraceptives will not provide this type of dual protection, which is why I do not think that sexually active single women should use the "pill" for contraception. It gives a flawed and false sense of confidence. Sure, you may not get pregnant, but STD is the bigger danger, and the "pill" offers no protection from that. If you are single and are having sex, I would strongly advise that you withdraw from the sexual part of the relationship. If you are not going to do that, you should at least protect yourself from *both* STD and pregnancy by using contraceptive foam and also insisting that your partner use condoms every time you have intercourse.

## Why Not Unmarried Mutual Monogamy?

If you are a virgin but anticipate having intercourse before you are married, you probably do not think that you would ever become promiscuous. You probably also believe that you would be at no real risk by having intercourse with only one guy. On both these points you may be right (at first), but this attitude could mark the beginning of a damaging downhill slide. Even though you don't initially plan to break up with that first man, you do break up. You don't plan to start having sex with the next guy you are close to, but the behavior you established with your first partner is so easily repeated. This is the dangerous but insidious deterioration I see occurring again and again in the lives of women who become sexually active outside of marriage.

Sexually transmitted disease is not spreading because of "promiscuous women" who are having sex with two or three different men every week. Sexually transmitted disease continues to be an epidemic in our country because of women who have sex with only one man this year, then sex with another man two years from now—and who repeat this pattern as the years go by. Although this is

---

**Lengthy monogamous relationships were not associated with a low incidence of infection.**

S. Sauls in *Medical Aspects of Human Sexuality*, 12/89

---

labeled mutual (unmarried) monogamy, I caution you that it is a lie to call such relationships "safe." Mutual monogamy is a major cause of the STD epidemic; it is not a solution for the epidemic and does not provide protection against STD.

You see, the problem is that once you have decided you are ready to give up your virginity outside of marriage, you have crossed a psychological barrier. The usual result is that from then on all close relationships you have with men will be sexual. You did not plan to establish that behavior pattern when you first had intercourse; you did not mean it to be that way, but that is what usually happens. (Even if you are mutually intending to marry each other "some day," there are no guarantees that this will happen!) When you are in an unmarried sexual relationship, that relationship will usually end by falling apart. When it does end, the woman is often left in ashes. If intercourse has become your pattern, when you get close to a man again, you will probably have sex with him also. And that relationship will probably end, leaving more of life's ashes for you. The final result is more broken sexual relationships and a huge bag full of ashes, a high chance of STD, moral compromise and probably guilt, and finally emotional hardness and bitterness. After several years of this behavior, you may finally discover that one-man-in-a-million for you, and you marry him. You then enter marriage dragging that dusty bag of past behavior. Is it any wonder that so many marriages start off on shifting sand instead of on a strong, rock-hard foundation?

In the many discussions of how to prevent sexually transmitted diseases, the encouragement to engage in nonmarital mutual monogamy is the worst deception of all. Some so-called experts make a mutually faithful relationship sound so safe, so warm, and so appealing. Nothing could be farther from the truth. Statistics show very clearly: *It is the number of sexual partners one has in a lifetime that affects the probability of contracting an STD,* not whether each of those relationships was mutually monogamous at the time. An excellent study done several years ago showed that when people had ten or more sexual partners in their lifetime, the chances of having contracted the hepatitis B virus were increased enormously over those who had fewer sex partners.

## Implications

Sometimes I find it hard to get patients to understand the danger of mutual monogamy. One of my patients, thirty-year-old Susan, is a typical example. We discussed the fact that she changes sexual partners about once a year. She insisted, "I'm not promiscuous. I only have intercourse with one man over a period of time." Yet Susan was in my office because she had an abnormal Pap smear. There were precancerous changes on her cervix caused by the venereal wart virus (HPV). Whether or not she considered herself promiscuous, she had nevertheless contracted a sexually transmitted disease.

This dangerous "safe" feeling is prevalent. People who have intercourse with "only one person at a time" do not consider themselves promiscuous and, therefore, feel they are not likely to acquire a sexually transmitted disease. This assumption is simply not true. Men and women who base their sexual behavior on this premise are at great risk of STD infection.

Considering the correlation between STD and promiscuity, a person who changes sexual partners every two or three years may as well have intercourse with all those people during the same night. It is just as potentially harmful to switch partners every year or two as it is to have sex with many different people during that same period of time.

Unmarried mutual monogamy is not the answer. The use of condoms is not an answer. The terms "safe sex" and "safer sex" are misleading, although the words themselves can make you believe your risks are low if you are using those techniques. If "safe sex" methods do not really provide protection, what does? Read on.

# 4

# Is Marriage the Answer?

SO-CALLED SAFE-SEX TECHNIQUES have actually contributed to the increased spread of sexually transmitted disease rather than helping to solve the problem. Likewise, the call to mutually faithful (nonmarital) sexual relationships as a cure-all has made people *feel* more safe but has been a major factor in the rampant spread of STD. As a single, you may look at these facts and ask, "Is there no answer? Am I destined to abstain from all sex in the future if I want to be healthy and safe?"

No, this is not the only solution. There is one that has been patiently waiting in the wings, a neglected "hero" that is finally allowed to come on the scene and save the day. This alternative, which more and more people are adopting, is "mutually faithful marriage." What people are rediscovering about marriage is that it can be a safe harbor in the midst of the storms of life, including the threat of sex-related disease. In a marriage relationship, two people form a closed circle into which STD cannot enter as long as each remains faithful. The marriage bond creates a hedge around two private lives behind which they can exhilarate in the luxury and privilege of a sexual freedom that cannot exist in any other environment. They can pleasure each other as they spend years experimenting with and exploring their sexual relationship, secure in the knowledge that they need fear neither sexual exploitation by the other nor sexually transmitted disease.

Before I go any further, I want you who are single women to know that I am sensitive to your dilemma. Many of you desire marriage, but it just hasn't happened. Many of you are not having sex because you believe that sex outside of marriage is not healthy (or smart). In that case, I would encourage you to accept your single condition and move on in life. Do a good job at your profession; get involved in local charities; reach out to needy people. There are many opportunities to live a full life even though unmarried and not sexually active. To those of you who have *chosen* to remain single, I would also explain that I have included this chapter because marriage seems to have acquired a bad reputation in our society. And it is not nearly as bad a deal as many think! As a matter of fact, marriage is a very good deal. Those who have been purposely avoiding it should relax and not worry so much about whether or not to join the ranks of the married. Bear with me, please, whatever your views about marriage. Maybe the good things I say about marriage will influence even the most staunch advocate of the single state.

Lest you think I am exaggerating the blessings of marriage, the national news media reported February 14, 1990—Valentine's Day—on a study showing that 90 percent of husbands and wives had never cheated on their partners since they had married. That statistic is probably true, because the same report said that most married people surveyed consider their marriage partner their best friend.

A second report showed much the same thing. Columnist Abigail Van Buren, in June 1988, in response to a question she posed to her readers, "Have you cheated on your mate?" received some surprising answers. About 85 percent of the women and 74 percent of the men claimed they had been faithful in marriage. (A total of 210,336 readers responded to her question.) The *Austin American Statesman* reported that the extent of fidelity astonished even Van Buren. They quote her as saying, "I learned that we are a far more moral society than most people thought." I would say that it also showed that married people like being married! These findings are very encouraging to those debating whether or not marriage is a good idea.

I am definitely not naive about marriage, and I know there are failures. Any gynecologist who listens to his or her patients hears the heartbreak of women who have suddenly, without warning, been left by their husbands. We sense the emotional and physical pain of the woman who discovers that the genital sore she has is herpes, which has come from a husband who had an affair. We also agonize for the man whose wife is emotionally withdrawing from him and finally leaves him and their children for a "fool's paradise" with another man. Marriages are not perfect and never will be—because people are imperfect beings. But marriage is light-years better than any of the other sexual alternatives available to us.

## The Plus Side of Marriage

Since marriage has received a huge amount of bad press in recent years (much of it undeserved), let me share some startling information about marriage that may greatly surprise you.

First, people are much more satisfied in marriage than we are led to believe by divorce statistics and TV soap operas. I have already cited the study reporting that most married people consider their marriage partner their best friend. Pollster Louis Harris reported in 1988 that when he talked to three thousand married couples, 89 percent of them said that the relationship with their partner was satisfying. Similarly, a Gallup poll done that year questioned one thousand women aged 18 to 44. About 53 percent of the married women reported being "very satisfied" with their lives, compared to 28 percent of the unmarried women. (It is interesting that married women with children were even more likely to be satisfied with their lives.)

A second positive finding about married people is that they are healthier than the unmarried (independent of sexually transmitted disease). The *Saturday Evening Post* (Jan./Feb. 1990) reported: "The new evidence linking health to marriage and family life is voluminous. Writing recently in *Social Science and Medicine,* Catherine Riessman and Naomi Gerstel note that one of the most consistent observations in health research is that married people enjoy better health than those of other marital statuses! Drs. Riessman and Gerstel note that compared with married men and women, the divorced, single, and separated suffer much higher rates of disease, morbidity, disability, mental neuroses, and mortality." The *Saturday Evening Post* went on to quote Peggy A. Thoits of Indiana University:

> Married persons have significantly lower anxiety and depression scores than unmarried persons, regardless of gender. Dr. Thoits notes that the married appear to enjoy better mental health even when they have experienced more potentially traumatic experiences than the unmarried.

Another article that emphasizes the same truth was published in *Physician and Patient* (June 1984) and titled, "The Ripple Effect of a Satisfying Marital Relationship." The author, Domeena Renshaw, M.D., indicated that married people live longer and healthier lives. The article stated that the ripple effect of a satisfying marriage provides a person with stability, security, satisfaction, love, and self-esteem. Renshaw ended by saying, "Affection, love, laughter, talking and touching all help build trust."

This may be why a survey done in 1985 by the Roper organization for Virginia Slims also showed surprising results. This survey, which had been tracking the progress of women in society for fifteen years, found that only 4 percent of women and 6 percent of men thought either cohabitation or living alone was the most satisfying lifestyle. Almost all men and women surveyed thought that marriage is the most satisfying way of life.

Finally, one of the most startling facts about marriage is discovered by examining a modern myth. We have all heard that one-half of all marriages end in divorce—a depressing statistic for those considering marriage but a statistic that I am happy to report is not true. Louis Harris, the pollster cited earlier, found that only one in eight marriages ends in divorce. He quotes 1981 figures from the National Center for Health Statistics, showing that there were 2.4 million marriages and 1.2 million divorces. But in 1981 there were 54 million marriages *already* existing in this country. In other words, only 2 percent of all the marriages then in existence actually ended in divorce that year. Since 1981 there has actually been a decline in the U.S. divorce rate.

Another reason why statistics seem to show that so many marriages end in divorce is that people whose first marriage ends in divorce often marry and divorce two or three times (or more), causing the statistics and the conclusions to be distorted.

## Minimizing the Effects of the Past

An attitude I frequently find, especially among younger people, is "If I have already had sex or if the guy I love has already had sex with someone else, why should I wait until marriage to have intercourse?" Remember, the ideal is that neither partner has had sex before marriage. I don't want to dilute that message, but it is only realistic to recognize that many people have sex while they are single. If you are one of those individuals, remember that the more sexual partners you and your future husband have had, the greater the chance that each of you now has a form of STD. The clear message is: "The fewer sexual partners you have ever had, the better for your future happiness and health." So, just because you have had intercourse in the past, don't feel that you may as well continue having sex as a single, even with the man you think you may marry eventually.

When you mutually decide to marry, you could have an STD if you have had sex before. Except for AIDS, most of these diseases can be treated or tolerated and, with the right attitude of understanding and love and patience, most infections need not be a stumbling block in your marriage. In a faithful marriage relationship, the husband and wife no longer risk being infected by other sexual partners. They can usually get control of any STD already existing when they married. There are certain recommendations I would make, however.

First, before you marry, both of you should be tested for STD if you have had intercourse with others. Even if only one of you has had intercourse with another person—and during your dating before marriage the two of you have had sex—I still recommend that both of you have testing done. This screening should include blood tests for syphilis, AIDS, and hepatitis B. It is advisable that you both be cultured for gonorrhea and chlamydia and that you be tested for trichomonas as well.

Since AIDS cannot be cured, if one of you has that terrible disease, the other person must then decide if he or she wants to go through with the marriage. This can be a very difficult decision, of course.

If one person is a carrier of hepatitis B, as a couple you would want to consult with an infectious-disease specialist to learn about vaccination against hepatitis B and the long-term consequences of this disease. I would recommend this prior to marriage.

Although gonorrhea and chlamydia can be treated, an infected woman would not know if she had been made infertile by either disease. I would not recommend infertility testing just because you were found to harbor these organisms, since they may not have affected your fertility.

About 15 percent of all married couples have a fertility problem for any of several reasons. If you do not become pregnant after trying for one year, you would want to consult an infertility specialist, whether or not you knew you had once been infected with chlamydia or gonorrhea. It takes an operation called a laparoscopy to tell if the fallopian tubes have been damaged by chlamydia or gonorrhea. If infection has caused you to be infertile, good medical care can often solve that. Adoption or in vitro fertilization, of course, can be an answer.

If either of you has herpes I can understand the turmoil you feel. Just having herpes can be embarrassing. It is a constant reminder of previous sexual encounters. Though you may always experience a whisper of anxiety about its presence, I would encourage you to have joyful intercourse with your spouse and not worry about the possibility that the uninfected partner will contract the herpes. During the years of marriage, if one partner is susceptible and the other partner has herpes, the uninfected one will eventually get herpes anyway. There is no way to avoid this. Since herpes is not dangerous and, after the first episode, is not especially painful, there is no reason to let herpes ruin the sexual pleasure that is so much a part of a good marriage. The only time there is real danger from herpes is if a woman has an outbreak of the virus while delivering a baby. Herpes transmitted to a newborn can be very serious.

If either one of you has been infected with venereal warts, get them treated. If you get married before they are all cleared up, use foam and condoms until neither of you has had any warts for six months. Possibly you will both be free of warts from then on. I mentioned earlier that the virus causing these warts can cause cancer of both the male and female genital organs. If *either* of you has had an HPV infection, I recommend that you be sure to have a Pap smear and pelvic exam done every year. If your husband develops any growth on his penis or scrotum, he should be examined immediately.

With these precautions, a couple can get married and feel comfortable about any STD they may have had (except for AIDS). Then, as a faithful married couple, they never have to worry about any new STDs. That's why it is best not to have sex until marriage. Even if you are not a virgin, however, you can still get married and have a healthier and happier life than if you continued having sex outside a marriage relationship.

## Implications

Let's recap the information about marriage. First, in today's world it is the only sensible option for a person who wants to enjoy sex but avoid a sexually transmitted disease. Though you should never enter marriage just to have sex, if you marry the right person with the right attitude you can enter a relationship with a person of the opposite sex that fulfills most of the innermost needs of the human heart. Marriages must be doing a good job at this—we have just seen that most married people are faithful to each other throughout marriage. They have never cheated on their partner and probably never will.

Second, we have seen that most people are satisfied with their marital status and consider their marriage partner their best friend.

Third, we have learned that marriage is good for the body; that married people are healthier than the non-married.

Finally, and most startling of all, we have seen that contrary to what we have always been taught, most married people *never* get divorced.

Why does marriage work? Domeena C. Renshaw, M.D., (professor in the department of psychiatry at Loyola University of Chicago, and director of the Sexual Dysfunction Clinic), in the previously cited article, says that "marriage offers sexual fulfillment, security and freedom from loneliness. Good marriages hold promise of an involved partner at one's side, plus an opportunity to build the kind of special home atmosphere most people believe is ideal." She names a number of benefits marriage has, including:

1. *Continuity*—self-perpetuation through offspring
2. *Stability*—a true sense of permanence and place
3. *Security*—feeling safe in being yourself
4. *Satisfaction*—attaining a union with another that cures the aloneness felt so acutely by many people
5. *Loving sex*
6. *Self-esteem*—positive feedback is given and received
7. *Anger safety valve*—a secure home is a safe place to express all feelings honestly
8. *A private bond*—the marital pact extends the self-concept from "I" to "we"

# 5

# Realities About Men, Women, and Sexuality

FOR THE ENTIRE period of the "sexual revolution" of the past thirty years, certain experts have been saying that all sex—married or unmarried—is okay, if the partners are responsible, thoughtful, and considerate of each other. These standards do not seem to be adequate. Sexual freedom has certainly not worked for the benefit of women. As a matter of fact, the results of this sexual license have been so devastating to womankind that they caused James O. Mason, former director of the Centers for Disease Control, to say in a speech a few years ago, "Sometimes I wonder why the female population does not stand up and scream about this."

Do you know what James O. Mason would want women to scream about? He might want them to complain bitterly about the ravages of STD on their bodies. But it does no good to rant and rave about disease. What women really need to complain about, what they need to protect themselves from, are the men who give them disease. This is much easier for me to say than for you to do. There are many reasons why you may find it terribly difficult to withhold yourself sexually from a man to whom you are not married. You *can* do this, however, and the rewards you will experience in later life will be so abundant and overwhelming that the memory of those difficult decisions will fade away into insignificance.

You can become confident that you are doing the sensible thing when you refuse to have intercourse until you are married, by learning some very important "facts of life." You can also be encouraged in this decision by listening to the voice of morality that is deep inside all of us and is always trying to get our attention. (We will first talk about the *facts* and talk more about *morality* in the next chapter.)

## Gender Differentials

The facts I want to discuss here concern the inherent differences in the way men and women are made. If you are knowledgeable about those differences, you will be more alert when a man tries to manipulate you into sexual activity that you might not want. If you assume that men think and feel and react exactly the way women do, you are a perfect mark, an ideal set-up to be used for his purposes. By understanding the very real differences in the way women and men perceive themselves, you can protect yourself from a man who wants to use you sexually. Some men would exploit you physically—leaving you with STD or pregnancy (or both) as well as deep emotional scars. Currently one of my associates is treating four unmarried fourteen-year-old girls, all of whom are infected with chlamydia.

Many problems can arise between men and women because what most women want in a relationship is intimacy on *all* levels, not just the physical. For men, however, the immediate and primary motivation is often only the sex act. This generalization is very bluntly stated, but it is almost universally true. I would not deny that women as well as men have sexual needs. But there are innate gender differences in the way sexuality and other human drives operate, based on both physiological makeup and certain culturally acquired behavior patterns that have defined the way women and men interact.

Lest you think I am "man bashing" let me state first that I believe man's so-called aggressiveness is part of his nature. Men have the hormone—testosterone—to make them more aggressive than women. For one thing, a man needs aggressiveness to approach a woman for the act of intercourse.

I believe men also *do* have as part of their inherent nature a desire and need for intimate warmth and love. But it seems probable that they learn a great deal about those qualities from women, whose physiological makeup and related drives center more on nurturing behavior.

If sex is part of a relationship *before* both partners have committed themselves to each other for life, a distortion of the man's expectations occurs. The specific result may be that the man's desire and hunger for the sex act totally consume his thoughts about this woman—and even all women. He has no incentive to learn to be nurturing and self-denying toward the woman he is close to if he has already learned that being manipulative and demanding can usually get him exactly what he wants. Once a man begins to relate to women in this fashion, he begins feeling deep inside that one of the worst things that can happen in any relationship is for the woman to deny him sex.

To make sure that a woman does not withhold herself from him, a man may resort to intimidating and sometimes very scary behavior. Even if he does not actually use physical methods of "persuasion" (and some men do, of course), other manipulative techniques, though more subtle, can be almost as effective in getting the man the sex he wants.

I do not want to give the impression that all males engage in premarital sex. They do not. A man is absolutely normal if he chooses to wait until marriage before he has sex. Many thoughtful, responsible men respect women, treat them that way, do not have the ulterior motive of manipulating a date to have sex, and do not plan to have sex till marriage.

Such men know that their sense of self-esteem does not depend on whether or not they have had sex with one or more girls. Sex is not the primary focus of their lives. I would encourage you to join the ranks of these men who show restraint, maturity, and self-confidence by deciding not to have casual sex. Many men today have multiple interests outside the sexual arena. They are vitally involved in these pursuits and are proving their self-worth with these interests. They find that living their life free of sexual involvement till marriage keeps their life much more fun, much more successful, and much more safe.

## Some Alarming Statistics

In a study at the University of Connecticut, reported in 1986 by D. L. Mosher and R. E. Anderson (*Journal of Research in Personality* 20:77), it was found that most of the seventy-five middle-class nineteen-year-old males with whom they talked had used force or other exploitation to achieve sex with their dates. Two out of three reported having gotten a woman drunk for that purpose. More than half had arranged to enter a date's apartment "so I could get her where I wanted her," as one man commented.

In addition, over 40 percent had sought to intimidate their dates with verbal manipulation—"I have told a woman that her refusal to have sex with me was changing the way I felt about her." Or threatened rejection: "I have gripped a woman tightly and given her an angry look when she was not giving me the sexual response I wanted." Other scientific studies have shown similar results. If you are realistic about men, you will understand that some of them will try to intimidate a woman mentally or emotionally to attain sexual capitulation.

Even worse are men who force themselves on women. The term *date rape* has been applied to this act, and rightly so.

Mosher and Anderson found that almost 20 percent of their subjects had actually used physical strength to force a date to have sex or frightened her into compliance by displays of violence. Similarly, a 1987 article in *The Archives of Sexual Behavior* (vol. 16, no. 2) by Angelynne Amick and Karen S. Calhoun cited "the alarmingly widespread nature of sexual victimization among university students. Although the vast majority of these women failed to label themselves as rape victims, 58 percent had experienced sexual intercourse against their will. . . . Certainly sexual victimization is a very significant, although often hidden, phenomenon among these students."

In a report entitled "Nonconsensual Sex on the College Campus: A Common Occurrence," Michael Clay Smith in *Clinical Practice in Sexuality* (vol. 4, no. 4) states,

> Emerging data reveal that forcible sexual intercourse— often perpetrated by a voluntary social companion—is becoming a shockingly frequent phenomenon on America's campuses. Campus administrators, student counselors, and campus security officials have just begun to recognize the magnitude of the problem and to respond to the damage it does to institutional morale and image as well as to the victims.

Mary P. Koss of Kent State University, after surveying seven thousand college students, reported in *MS* magazine (Oct. 1985) that 51 percent of the women surveyed had experienced some form of sexual victimization less than rape or attempted rape, and almost 90 percent of such victims knew their assailants. In addition, Koss found that one-quarter of the female students had been the victims of either rape or attempted rape, and 8 percent had actually been raped, according to the legal definition. (Of particular interest is that almost three-quarters of the women raped did not recognize their experience as legally defined rape. Likewise, while one in every twelve men surveyed admitted to having fulfilled the definition of rape or attempted rape, virtually none considered himself a "rapist.")

Michael Smith (in "Nonconsensual Sex on the College Campus") writes:

> Date rape refers to situations in which the perpetrator and victim were voluntarily in each other's company, but the victim did not consent to sexual behavior going as far as it did—to sexual penetration. Those who have researched the phenomenon have found that victims, often, did not know that such a forced act constitutes legal rape. It clearly does. Likewise, the aggressors often did not realize their forced attentions could land them in jail.

As a result of their study, Amick and Calhoun suggested several methods of preventing "date rape," the first of which is "educating women about the prevalence of acquaintance victimization, rather than having victims learn by experience as did many of our successful resisters."

I remember very clearly one young woman who suffered the trauma and bitter aftermath of "date rape." She was a coed at a local university and came to me because she thought she was pregnant. After I confirmed her fears, she told me of the night she became pregnant. She had been looking forward to her date with one of the university's football players but was a virgin and did not plan to have intercourse that night. Before she realized what was happening, the man physically forced her to have intercourse against her will. She never saw him again and because of embarrassment did not prosecute him as the rapist he was. I wish she had.

## The Subtleties of Sexual Pressuring

Other forms of victimization are less obvious than actual or attempted rape. Various manipulative techniques may be used by a man whose aim is to achieve sexual intimacy. He may lie about his past and present sexual experience, and even about the existence of a sexually transmitted disease, if he believes that bending the truth will gain compliance. An inexperienced woman may be deceived into having sex, simply because the man vows that she is "the first" or "really special." If a woman desires intercourse with a particular man, she, too, may use lying or other forms of manipulation to seduce him.

Psychologist Susan D. Cochran of California State University, Northbridge, surveyed 660 people in 1989. About 47 percent of the men and 42 percent of the women said they had told dates they had fewer previous sexual partners than they actually had. In addition, 42 percent of the men and 33 percent of the women said they would not tell a date if they had had a one-night stand. Also, 23 percent of the men and 10 percent of the women said they would not admit that they were currently involved with someone else.

> *For the sake of your self-respect and your health, avoid being manipulated. Almost any man who is trying to persuade or intimidate you into having sex is probably sexually experienced and therefore quite likely to have an STD.*

I had a patient for whom it was a very unpleasant surprise to learn that her sexual partner had a past life that she had not known about. Many would consider her a responsible and cautious single adult. She had had sex with only two men in her thirty-five years of life. But she recently got herpes from one of them. She had thought her new boyfriend was a conservative and generally moral man. When she confronted him with the news about her herpes, he confessed that when he was in college, he had sometimes participated in group sex.

Some men will even lie about having a sexually transmitted disease if they think a woman might deny them sex if they knew it. In one study of men being tested for AIDS (done by Susan M. Keeglas, Ph.D., and colleagues at the University of California, San Francisco), 12 percent said they would not tell their primary partner if they were found to have AIDS. About 25 percent said they would not tell a secondary partner. Yet these men knew that passing AIDS to another person would be a death sentence! If some men would lie about having AIDS, they would certainly lie about having other, less frightening diseases.

There is another aspect to this. Men for centuries have been pledging their love to women, hoping to be rewarded with sexual favors. Without seriously intending to marry, some men ask women to marry them so the woman will allow sexual activity. Remember, the way a man proves his authentic love to a woman is to marry her. You should consider any other pledge of love as counterfeit until authenticated by marriage. For the sake of your self-respect and your health, avoid being manipulated. Almost any man who is trying to persuade or intimidate you into having intercourse is probably sexually experienced and is therefore quite likely to have an STD.

Of course, many men would not lie about such an important matter. You might feel very confident that your special somebody would always tell you the truth about his sexual background or anything else, for that matter. But you cannot be sure. However, even if he is truthful, remember that up to 70 percent of people infected with STD do not know it.

You also need to examine your own motives and be honest about your relationship with men. Some women pressure a man into having intercourse with them, often with the mistaken notion that sexual activity seals their mutual commitment and thus will win his permanent allegiance. Others, men and women alike, simply hope to prove they are "modern" by adopting behavior that rejects what some people consider outdated and overly restrictive sexual standards. Charlene L. Muehlenhard, in *Medical Aspects of Human Sexuality* (April 1989), showed this very clearly:

Do men ever have sex against their will with women? Our recently completed study shows that the answer is a resounding Yes. In our sample population of almost 1,000 undergraduate students, 62.7 percent of the men reported that they participated in unwanted sexual encounters.

What motivated these men to take part in sexual activities they did not want? Our questionnaire revealed that virtually none was physically forced. Most of these men blame "pressure," sometimes from the woman or from their peers, but often they blame what they consider to be society's prevailing sexual expectations for men. While society expects women not to be too sexually active or to agree to sex too readily, its traditional "double standard" indicates that men should be sexually experienced and use sexual opportunities whenever they arise.

The most common pressuring device that the men reported was "enticement"—"The woman started taking off the man's clothes or her own, or tried to sexually stimulate him by touching him." One man in this situation said, "Face it. Men are trapped. If a woman makes an advance, a man can't say no, or she'll think there's something wrong with him." Indeed, verbal "coercion" was a common technique used by women to obtain sex: "The partner had said that everybody does it, had questioned their sexuality by implying that they were 'impotent,' had made them feel guilty, or had said that it was now or never." Intoxication played a large role in many of these situations. A young man I know has chosen not to have sex until he is married. Yet one of his dates accused him of being homosexual when he rejected her sexual advances.

It may seem difficult to grasp the idea that both men and women may feel pressured into having sex. Considering the difficulty with communication between the sexes, however, it is not hard to understand that a man may imagine that any warmth or closeness a woman shows is an indication that she wants to have sex. On the other hand, a woman may feel so certain that every man she dates wants to have intercourse that she entices or initiates the action and a man feels pressured to cooperate.

## Wary, Wise—and Safe

Now that I have been "fair" and discussed the fact that men, too, have been victims of sexual aggression, let us return to the original premise that men are, *for the most part*, more physically aggressive and sexually demanding. And women, *for the most part*, are more often the victims of those demands.

One explanation for the victimization of women by aggressive males is that women like affectionate closeness, including touching and caressing, in and of itself. They may engage in what amounts to foreplay without the least intention of having intercourse. A man's thoughts are often far different. A 1984 article reported in *The Archives of Sexual Behavior* (113, no. 3), by Nancy Wadsworth Denney, Jeffrey K. Field, and David Quadagno, stated that "while females report wanting more foreplay, when males were asked, 'Are physical affection and touching important for their own sakes, not leading to orgasm or even necessarily to sex?' a large majority of men answered that physical affection should always eventually lead to intercourse and orgasm." Some of their comments were:

> "Affection, touching, hugging, talking, kissing are all meaningless and uninteresting unless there is at least some hope that they will eventually lead to sex."
> "I don't like playing around for nothing."
> "Affection is important in the early stage of life, but as far as affectionate sex, that is childish. Sex is not meant for affection. It is a release of pressure, and every man has his own level of how much pressure he can stand."

All the students quoted above were single, and in my opinion and in the opinion of most psychologists, they are wrong. But this is the type of man you might find yourself alone with. You need to be wise and wary, for your own protection. Another way to state this was reported in the *Austin American Statesman* (Feb. 27, 1990). A University of New Hampshire study done by Barbara Montgomery, chairwoman of the university's communications department, concluded that: "Men and women understand flirtation differently. Men tend to see it as a prelude to physical intimacy, while women regard it as a way to establish friendship."

What is the solution to the problem that men are sexually aggressive and women receptive? Is intercourse an inevitable result of any modern relationship, regardless of moral or any other constraints, including the danger of disease? I do not believe this is so. Men and women are not animals who must blindly follow their urges. Men can consciously limit their sexual aggressiveness, just as women can choose to control their responsiveness to men.

## Implications

Women have far more to lose in this, one of humanity's longest lasting dilemmas. Except for AIDS, men usually suffer very little from the effects of most STDs and never become pregnant. It is my opinion that womankind must resume the role they relinquished about thirty years ago—that of setting the standards for sexual activity in the male/female relationship. I strongly encourage you to avoid sex until you are married. If you are involved sexually with a man now, that relationship has a near 100 percent chance of breaking up. If and when it does, I highly recommend that you not get involved sexually with the next man you get close to until he marries you. Many men will avoid marital bonding as long as they can. If they can have what they want without assuming the obligations of marriage, a number of men will sidestep that commitment as long as they can.

Some women have the mistaken idea that if they let a man they love start having sex with them, his affection will grow deeper and they will eventually marry. This is reverse thinking and is a sure recipe for disaster. A good example of this occurred with a patient of mine who had begun having sex with her boyfriend in the belief that they would some-day be married. When he continued to find reasons to put off the marriage date, she became more and more uncom-fortable about their relationship and began to wonder if she was being exploited. He eventually left her, and she bears physical and emotional scars that will last a lifetime. I have heard this scenario time and again.

If you think clearly about this, you will realize that if you allow sexual intimacy, you cancel one masculine incentive for getting married. The guy may truly love you and want to be close to you through intercourse, but you can let him know that he can have that and more the day he marries you—and not a day before. You do have this power and I would urge you to use it. In this way, you both are assured of getting what is the basis of any sound and lasting rela-tionship—commitment, intimacy, affection, family, and the opportunity to give fully of yourselves for the sake of the other. This is the best for you—and it is the best for him.

Because marriage testifies to a mutual lasting commitment, in no other relationship in life is there so much freedom, both emotional or sexual. The opposite side of the coin is summed up by Pepper Schwartz, a sociologist from the University of Washington: "Men are more non-monogamous because there are more women willing to be non-monogamous with them." Women have the power to change this, and they should now have the motivation to do so.

# 6

# Debunking the Myths
# of "Liberated Sex"

PRIOR TO THE mid-1950s, there was relatively little threat from sexually transmitted disease. There was no AIDS to worry about; herpes was uncommon; chlamydia was very rare. Although gonorrhea and syphilis had been on the scene for decades, both were curable with one penicillin injection.

The main reason these diseases were so uncommon before the so-called sexual revolution was that men and women did not generally have intercourse with each other until they were married. And, once married, few people had extramarital affairs. Obviously, there had always been exceptions, but they happened so infrequently that neither STD nor pregnancy in single women was much of a problem.

I have found that people who became adults during the 60s, 70s, and 80s find it hard to believe that their elders really lived that way. I assure you that they did! The low incidence of STD and the low pregnancy rates in nonmarried women prove it. Remember, too, that so far as pregnancy is concerned, those were the days before abortion was legalized and became a common practice. If a single woman became pregnant, most people knew about it.

Despite today's alarming statistics, you can, as a single, live free from the dangers of STD and the concern about pregnancy. You can have your own safe harbor by following the ideas in this book.

Is it realistic for me to suggest to you that there is a way out of the confusing sexual maze that involves your male friends' expectations, peer pressure, and the threat of disease or unwanted pregnancy? Yesterday I performed a very difficult operation on a woman in an attempt to repair her reproductive organs, terribly damaged by an STD that has caused her twelve years of infertility. Later, I was talking about STD with the anesthesiologist. He asked, "Is it realistic to tell people that they need to stop changing sexual partners and stay with only one partner the rest of their lives?" Let me add that he is a young doctor, a very moral man, who married just a few years ago. He and his wife recently had a beautiful baby boy. He was not saying, "*I* am going to have an affair" but implying, "Isn't it idealistic to talk about a lifetime partner for all those other people in our country? They probably don't have the good sense I do about this problem!"

Because I am not naive, I know that some of you will not believe what I am trying to get you to hear. You are already convinced that your boyfriend could not have STD or that you are not promiscuous (because you have sex with just one man over a period of time) or that since he uses condoms, you could not become pregnant or get an STD. Remember, if you do not have an STD now, you will probably get an STD in the future. My most fervent hope for you is that AIDS will not be your first such disease or that you will not become sterile from that first STD.

My related hope is that, *after* you get an STD, you will remember the ideas contained in this book and follow the suggestions I make in the rest of this chapter so you will never get an STD again. If you are a virgin, let the words of this book also be a forewarning that motivates you to erect a protective wall between you and all that STD that is out there.

Based on irrefutable evidence, it *is* realistic to tell people to avoid sexual activity outside of marriage. More than that, it is the only sensible approach for achieving healthy, unencumbered, uncomplicated sexual freedom and joy.

## Society's Distorted Message

The last thirty years—the period of the sexual "convulsion" (I prefer that term, rather than sexual "revolution") —have misled many people to believe that indiscriminate sex is normal for humans. I would encourage you to think otherwise, for several very important reasons.

Without doubt sex is one of the premier experiences of life. It is also a necessary physical drive, since no species would survive without it. Yet the way many humans have been practicing sex during the past few decades has produced untold misery, sterility, and even death. Sex has become like the poison a deranged man poured on the roots of the beloved Treaty Oak in Austin, Texas, a poison that sapped the tree of its beauty and health and probably its life. We, the people of this country, have been the deranged ones. We have poured the toxins of unrestricted sexuality on each other, robbing our lives of happiness, undermining our morality, destroying our ability to reproduce, and endangering our lives.

These thirty years have been a grotesque distortion in the sexual history of our society. This period of sexual excess does not represent what is normal. But now, increasing knowledge of STD is affecting the sexual activity of many people, and I hope you will let this information guide you. Below are some illustrations of how the sexual "revolution" is collapsing on itself.

Phil Kushin, in an article in *Potential* (Sept.-Oct. 1989), says: "There is much evidence that sexual attitudes and behavior have become more conservative over the last decade, a trend that appeared to begin even before AIDS started making national headlines in 1985."

In 1980, *Cosmopolitan* reported of one of its sex surveys that "so many readers wrote negatively about the sexual revolution, expressing longings for vanished intimacy, and the now elusive joys of romance and commitment, that we began to sense that there might be a sexual counter-revolution underway in America."

"Swinging couples are dwindling. Now, married people who are sexually bored of each other are searching out help to restore some excitement to their relationship. They don't want to go outside marriage for new sex partners because now it is a dangerous world out there" (Dr. Helen Singer Kaplan, director of the Human Sexuality Program at New York Hospital, Cornell Medical Center).

"I think AIDS is going to force women to profoundly re-think their sexuality. In recent years, women have wanted men to take equal responsibility for birth control and other sexual issues. This disease puts the burden back on them to take care of themselves" (Lauren Gordon, social worker at Montefiore Medical Center in the Bronx, in a *US* article, April 26, 1986).

What some people are still doing, however, is ignoring the way a human body is meant to function. In earlier times most women had the joy of sexually flourishing in the security of a marriage in which they knew they were not judged on "performance." In today's short-term, uncommitted relationships, either partner feels free to leave if the other person falls short of his or her expectations.

Prior to the last few decades, most men married. If they did not, they did without sex—simple as that! There have always been advantages available to a man in marriage, though he may not know that beforehand. If he can have the sexual pleasures of marriage without the responsibility, he may never sort out those other benefits—and you both will be losers in the long run.

## Weighing Your Options

What can you do? How should you respond to all this distressing information in the light of your own desires, pressure from a man you like to be with, and a still-distorted cultural message?

First, I encourage you to visualize the reality of the dangers of indiscriminate sex. Up to this point, I have concentrated on the physical dangers. Remember that so-called "safe" sex practices and limiting intercourse to only one person (but changing partners every few years) do not guarantee disease prevention. They are only smoke screens, hiding the lurking dangers of STD. There is almost no doubt that you will get an STD if you start having sex outside of marriage! The only real safety lies in having sex with one healthy person for life.

---

**The pregnancy rate for teenagers on birth-control pills is 18 percent.**

---

### Teenage Sexuality

Especially for teenagers, unmarried sex can also cause emotional turmoil. One study showed that teenagers who begin having sex outside of marriage develop feelings of guilt, regret, anxiety, and low self-esteem. Such teens often become promiscuous and encounter subsequent sexual problems.

Although an uncommitted relationship may look especially attractive to a young woman or man who is not yet ready for marriage, early sexual activity can cause severe problems for young people. Besides risking unwanted pregnancy and sexually transmitted disease, teenage couples who begin having sex often find it leading to too-early marriage, which may result in school drop-outs. Needless to say, those teenagers then face limited employment opportunities and future economic problems. Finally, teenagers who marry are three times more likely to divorce or separate, and those who become pregnant as teenagers have higher chances of a difficult pregnancy and delivery. Often, a complicated mix of emotions begins brewing once the original decision is made to have sex before marriage, whatever the age of the participants.

*Live-In Relationships*

Many women who decide to have sex, and also desire some element of closeness, opt for a live-in relationship, believing that the emotional turmoil of nonmarital sex would be reduced in the laboratory of this "more secure" relationship. However, I believe we can safely assume that such a relationship will be burdened with tremendous emotional baggage. What do we find in live-in relationships? Although it is not surprising that it is usually sex that brings couples together in a nonmarital union, it may be news that sex is a major cause for their breaking up. In *Medical Aspects of Human Sexuality* (Aug. 1986, vol. 20), A. Pietropinto reported that sexual dissatisfaction is the leading cause of cohabitant break-ups.

A live-together arrangement may look peaceful from the outside, but that is rarely a true picture of the situation. In an article entitled, "Swinging—and Ducking—Singles" from *Time* magazine (Sept. 5, 1988), we read the following statements:

1. Psychologists and sociologists are finding that single couples can be surprisingly violent, especially those who set up housekeeping together before marriage. In almost two dozen recent studies, experts across the country estimate that an average of almost 30 percent of all unmarried individuals, whether dating, engaged, or living together, have been involved in physical aggression with the opposite sex.

2. Courtship violence is a more serious problem than spouse abuse in our society. Young people do not have the economic resources or power to get the help they need

(James Makepeace, professor of sociology at the College of St. Benedict in Minnesota).

    3. Most of the outbursts involve lower-level violence: pushing, shoving, or slapping. A small percentage of these couples engage in clashes that result in broken bones or hospitalization.

    4. When asked why singles stay in a stormy relationship, James Kovall, a therapist who counsels couples in Long Beach, CA, says, "To make a decision about leaving a relationship is extremely tumultuous because of the total sense of loss. Unwed couples also tend to hide their private violence from others—perhaps even more so than married."

If you are single and considering a live-in relationship with a person of the opposite sex you need to be aware of the problems that are so often part of such unions. I suggest you ask yourself, "Why should I get myself involved in such a relationship?" Life is too short for that kind of no-win situation."

There has been much debate in the national media on whether or not it is best for a couple to live together before they get married. The previously cited article by A. Pietropinto pointed out that research has shown that living together provides no subsequent benefits insofar as marital sexual satisfaction, openness of communication, emotional closeness, relationship stability, or reduced likelihood of divorce.

Dr. Joyce Brothers wrote in *Parade* magazine (Oct. 20, 1989):

> I have noticed that a growing number of liberated women—many of whom once would have favored living-together arrangements—have concluded that sharing bed and board with a male is just another rip-off. Even when there is full equality in the rooms where a couple live, once they step outside the front door, women are realizing the myth is shattered and the odds are tipped in the man's favor.
>
> Emotionally, many women seem to want and need more commitment than do many men, and some become disillu-

sioned by the disposable quality of sex and love that too
often seems thoughtless and without continuity. Many are
finding that, just as they become adjusted to a living
arrangement and press for more commitment, the man
becomes vague. When they want to have a child, they are
faced with the prospect of having one out of wedlock or
none at all. Some find that they eventually lose out to a
woman who has not become quite so familiar on a day-to-
day basis.

Entering a relationship that, by its very nature, is built on
lack of commitment is not the healthiest thing for either
women or men. We all like to feel that close friends will not
abandon us if we do something that offends them, and none
of us wants our acceptance to be based on performance.
Living together like this, however, is by definition a "perfor-
mance-related" arrangement. If one member does something that the other does not like, he or she can, and often
does, simply move out. Because there are "no strings,"
working on the problem seems like too much trouble. In a
marriage, break-ups happen too, but since the split is much
more difficult to accomplish, time and effort are usually
spent on reconciliation attempts.

Perhaps an example will illustrate those dynamics. Jane
and Pete are good friends of mine. During the time their
children were young, they decided that they did not love
each other anymore. They planned to divorce as soon as
their children were out of school. As the years went by,
however, Jane and Pete worked together to provide and
care for the children. In the process, they discovered that
they loved and needed each other. The kids are out of college now, but the couple is still married, and closer than
they have ever been.

In contrast to this happy outcome, if you have sex with a
man outside of marriage, you probably do it because you
feel that he is truly interested in you and loves you as you
love him. When the relationship fades and the man leaves,
you realize that he did not really love you. You were mere-

ly a convenient outlet for his own selfish drives. The emotional impact of this on your self-esteem and confidence can be devastating. Moreover, it can sour your opinion of all men and make it harder for you to establish the love, trust, and relaxed and joyful intimacy both you and your future husband will want when you marry.

### What Will You Do?

If you are young, you may never have experienced true pain—the kind of agony that makes you feel as if your heart is being torn apart. You can forestall at least a bit of that kind of experience. Life will seem kinder if you stay away from sexual activity that could bring an intensity of agony and pain. One of my staff recently commented, "The trouble is that many young people have never really experienced terrible pain in their lives. They don't know how bad it can be." I hope you are not a person who must experience what she was talking about before you believe it.

You are one of four different types of women right now: (1) You are single and having sex; (2) you have had sex with a man (or several men) in the past; (3) you have never had intercourse; (4) you are married.

If you are already involved in a nonmarital sexual relationship, I would encourage you to continue the relationship *without further intercourse until you are married*. I realize this is a very difficult decision, and you will probably hear lots of complaining from your partner. But it will accomplish two things. First, it will protect you from STD if he is also having (or has had) sex with another woman (or man) without telling you. It will also show if he is truly interested in *all* of you. Wouldn't it be nice to know you are loved not just for your body but for who you are as a whole person?

If you cannot convince your "significant other" to stop the sexual part of the relationship, and you continue to have intercourse but don't get married, you and he will almost certainly break up eventually—almost all non-married relationships do.

If that happens, you become a part of the second group I mentioned. For women who are not sexually involved now but have been in the past, I encourage a re-evaluation of your attitudes and behavior with men in light of the information contained in this book. The next time you get close to a man, don't have sex with him until he marries you. (Of course, if you don't want to marry him, don't ever have intercourse with him.)

To you in the third group, who have never had intercourse, I would say words that both warn and encourage. I warn you that men will try to manipulate you into bed, that your girlfriends may make fun of your decision to remain celibate, and that your doctor may not believe you are a virgin. But I also encourage you to do the right thing. If you will avoid intercourse until marriage, you will be forever grateful for your wise decision and justifiably proud of your strength of character.

That type of statement is often challenged by a question: "Is waiting until marriage to have sex a normal thing?" Some people use the term *celibacy* to refer to anyone who is not involved in a sexual relationship. More precisely, celibacy actually refers to an unmarried person. *Abstinence* is the proper general term to use for someone who is refraining from sexual intercourse. No matter which term we use, the question comes back: "Is it normal to go without intercourse

| These figures demonstrate potential for "Teen Aid Abstinence Program" used by two high schools: | | |
|---|---|---|
| | **Before Program** | **After Program** |
| **San Marcos, Calif.** | 147 pregnancies in 600 girls | 20 pregnancies |
| **Spur, Texas** | 11 pregnancies in 450 girls | 1 pregnancy |

until marriage?" I have found that even some otherwise well-informed people believe that somehow abstinence can be physically harmful.

Let me state clearly and simply that sexual abstinence until marriage, even for people who do not marry until they are in their thirties or forties, is not only "normal," it is the only way to stay healthy. As a matter of fact, the most dangerous situation would be for a person who did not marry until rather late in life to have multiple sexual partners during all the single years.

Following my speech at a recent women's conference, a single woman asked, "Since my divorce seven years ago, I have not had intercourse. Does it hurt me physically to live this way?" I assured her that absolutely no damage to her body would result from not having intercourse, and that, conversely, intercourse outside a marriage relationship was much more likely to damage her body (with sexually transmitted disease) and her mind (with psychological entanglements) than abstinence would. I further assured her that when and if she does marry again, she will be able to enjoy sexual relations in a normal, healthy fashion. *The "use it or lose it" cliché is a flippant statement that has no basis in fact.*

Many times a female patient has told me that she had agreed to intercourse because the man said he was so aroused that if they did not have sex, it would damage his testicles. I tell such women that the next time they hear that line, they need not feel any guilt at all about saying no. A man's body is not harmed at all in experiencing arousal that does not culminate in intercourse. If a man's male organs become too congested, he will have a nocturnal emission (wet dream), the body's way of relieving that type of congestion.

Further, the "use it or lose it" principle has no more truth for the man than it does for the woman. A man can be quite confident that even if he goes for years without having intercourse, he will be able to have intercourse in a normal way when he does get married. On the other hand, if he does have sex outside marriage, he can be damaged by sexually transmitted disease and by the psychological impact of the relationship. *A man is much more likely to have his body damaged by sex outside of marriage than he is by abstinence.*

Dr. Domeena C. Renshaw says in an article in *The Female Patient* that "Making love does not have to include sexual intercourse. Men, women, boys, and girls all deserve to learn this essential and fundamental aspect of relating intimately. Life offers endless, ongoing stresses, but it also offers many gratifications. The most important of these are relationships: first with self, then with family, then with friends." She also points out that "many persons handle voluntary celibacy healthily and quite happily. Sexual feelings occur naturally and recur cyclically, regularly, including during sleep."

Men and women who are celibate (or abstinent) will probably have thoughts about sex, dreams about sex, and interest in sex. This is healthy and normal. But *thinking* about these things—and even being aroused—does not cause physical harm if sex does not occur.

The idea of emotional damage for a sexually abstinent person seems to have evolved from the Freudian psychology that became especially popular after World War I. Part of Freud's doctrine was that sexuality is such an important aspect of human personhood that to limit its expression is to cause mental and emotional damage. Many groups in our society accept this philosophy as fact and are operating accordingly. Dr. Willard Gaylin, clinical professor of psychiatry at Columbia University Medical School and author of the book *Rediscovering Love*, says that Freud was wrong. He writes:

> It simply can't be true because while the lifting of sexual inhibitions has certainly occurred, we psychiatrists and psychoanalysts aren't begging for patients. There's no evidence that the amount of neuroses or psychoses in the population is any less than it ever was.
>
> As a matter of fact, if you had to take only measurable and empirical data, the only proven result so far of the

sexual revolution is the occurrence of two terrifying epidemics—AIDS and teenage unmarried pregnancies. There's also the rapid increase of other venereal diseases, which, at one time, we had anticipated having had stamped out by now. . . . So far, the empirical data on the sexual revolution is not very reassuring.

What we see, then, is that Freud's concept of human behavior has greatly contributed to the sexual problems of our society—joyless sex, unwanted pregnancies, physical disease, and even death because of AIDS. Freud did us a great injustice indeed!

## Intimacy Without Intercourse

We all need intimacy. We are a society of people who are lonely and desperately want closeness, but we have often confused sexual experience with intimacy. Sex is not true intimacy. It can be an important part of *marital* intimacy, but outside of marriage, sex becomes a poison that destroys the very seeds of male/female intimacy before they have a chance to sprout.

In an article published in *Adolescence* (Summer 1986, vol. 21, no. 82), Carol A. Darling and Kenneth Davidson, Sr. state:

> The sexual concerns reported by these young men and women point to an apparent failing of the sexual revolution. . . . A . . . result has been a preoccupation with the race toward sexual intercourse and the achievement of orgasm. In the process, sensuality, affection, and intimacy have been sidetracked.

Many studies seem to agree that when women seek out sex, they generally think they are doing it to gain total intimacy. In a 1985 report in *Archives of Sexual Behavior* (14:13), J. L. Carroll reported that 85 percent of the women surveyed said that love and commitment are always (or almost always) their primary motives for sexual activity. In contrast, 61 percent of the men said emotional involvement was never, or only sometimes, their prerequisite for having intercourse.

Nancy Dickinson, clinical director of the Human Sexuality Institute in Washington, D.C., says, "People are looking for acceptance. They are looking to be vulnerable without getting slam-dunked. Sex does not equal intimacy."

As a woman, you need to realize that sex represents true intimacy *only* in marriage and that you are in great danger of being "slam-dunked" if you try to achieve that kind of intimacy outside of marriage. If you are single, don't be afraid to admit your need for a friend who loves you unconditionally. Sometimes a woman friend can fulfill this emotional need. Whether you have one person or more as your close friend, and whether their gender is male or female, you do need someone who will allow you the freedom to fail. In this type of relationship you can feel safe in relying on a person who goes above and beyond the call of duty. And you will want to reciprocate in kind. One way this is manifested is through your communication dynamics. A "best friend" talks honestly but will listen to you and value your opinions, even when you disagree. The beauty of this type of relationship is that it is not demanding— each of you will want to become the intimate friend that the other person needs. If you have such a relationship with an eligible man and he does not demand sex, you may be establishing the kind of closeness that can lead to a good marriage, although this does not always happen. By keeping physical involvement from undermining your caring relationship, you and a man can be very good friends and reach a level of nonsexual affection that is very healthy and may lead to a permanent commitment.

Phil Kushin comments in his article "The Legacy of the Sexual Revolution" (*Potential*, Sept.-Oct. 1989):

> Instead of free sex, mental health professionals are emphasizing the importance of commitment and intimacy in relationships. . . . If Americans listen to this advice, it appears

that the sexual revolution's days are numbered. In its place may be the "intimacy revolution." Not as catchy perhaps, but if the experts are right, a lot more satisfying.

It seems obvious that women tend to feel the need for intimacy deeply, sometimes enough to give their bodies for it—only to be sadly disappointed when their precious gift is given outside the security of marriage. Men, on the other hand, may desperately need intimacy, too, but often don't recognize that need until they have accepted the mutually binding vows of a marriage relationship.

# 7

# How to Say No

"JUST SAY NO!" sounds so negative and oversimplified. But these words imply a positive outcome, though "no" is often difficult to verbalize. Saying no at the right time can keep you from being killed in an automobile driven by a drunk friend. Saying no can keep you from blowing your mind with drugs. And saying no can keep you from the problems brought about by nonmarital sex. How can you find the conviction to say no and the means to make your decision prevail?

1. *Be convinced that the issues discussed in this book are legitimate.* Then think about these issues and decide on the safest kind of action for *you.* That decision should be an emotional choice, not just an intellectual conclusion. I hope you decide now to avoid sex until you get married. If so, make this decision part of your intellect, your emotions, your will, and your spirit. Only then will you have the ingredients for the "true grit" of firm resolve. Once you have made this choice a part of your total being, you will be free of the negative aspects of saying no and will no longer have to wrestle with the decision. It is not that you

will never again face sexual temptations. There will be skirmishes, but the big battle is won.

2. *Find a good friend with the same resolve about sex.* I was recently talking with an acquaintance about sexuality and singles. She remembered that during her teenage years she had a close girlfriend with whom she shared the same values. They kept each other out of trouble. Whenever one would weaken, the other would be strong. This is one way a close friend can be invaluable. And even if a man drops you because you will not have sex with him, you will have a caring friend ready to help you pick up the pieces.

3. *Write out your decision about sex.* Put this reminder where you can see it every day, especially if you are undergoing a period of temptation. Make it a commitment of your life and keep reviewing it. (In the drawer of the desk on which I am writing is a sheet of paper on which I have listed the goals I have for my life. I see that sheet almost every day. It helps me maintain my course, just like a compass. You can do the same.)

4. *Develop self-esteem.* All of us sometimes find it difficult to stand up for what we believe. If you realize that you are a person of worth, with opinions of great value, you can develop a confidence in what you think and how you act. This will enable you to say no whenever someone tries to change your beliefs or negatively influence your behavior.

5. *Practice assertiveness.* Many people meekly surrender their independence when someone pressures them into doing something they know is wrong. If your moral decisions are being challenged, it's time to be assertive. Everyone has the right to make decisions concerning his or her own body, especially when one's health is at stake. It is also important to realize that the mind and heart *can* control the body's urges!

6. *Let your values be known to the men with whom you share a mutual attraction.* It is important, for example, for a man to know that you are not going to have intercourse until you marry. This sets his mind straight immediately. It can also

be a weapon against date rape, which sometimes occurs because a man misinterprets a woman's dress, smile, and gentle touch as signals that she wants to have sex, even though that may not be her intention. Early in a relationship, be assertive enough about not having intercourse until marriage that that man knows you mean "no," not "maybe" and not "try again later."

7. *Don't get involved with men who you suspect will try to have sex with you.* Sometimes you cannot tell, but most of the time you know in your heart if a man has more interest in your physical self than he does in you as a total person. You don't need that kind of hassle, even though it can cause you to tingle temporarily. Remember your resolve and get rid of him.

8. *Plan your times with a man.* Don't just "get together" and see what happens. I believe the times during which you are most likely to end up having unwanted sex are when you are with a guy and it is not really a formal date. Many people who become involved in sex did not mean to. They merely had no particular plans for the evening, and intercourse resulted. Plan your times together, with minimum time allowed for uninterrupted privacy.

9. *Avoid alcohol and drugs.* I have already mentioned the association of alcohol and drugs with sexual activity. Many men use these substances to get a woman into bed with them. Alcohol and drugs deaden the mind and therefore the resolve. The solution seems simple—don't drink or use

> **It is important that teachers and parents tell young people that they should not have sex until they get married, just as teachers and parents are now telling young people they should not smoke and should not use drugs.**

drugs with a man, especially if you are suspicious of his intentions.

10. *Limit the amount of physical contact.* No matter how assertively you have said no, if you let a man have some freedom with your breasts or access into your clothes, he is going to think you really do want to have intercourse. At that point, you may not be able to stop him, since men are almost always physically stronger than women. I suggest that you never let him get started believing you might comply. You, the woman, must set the limits. You have that right. Unfortunately, even some well-intentioned and moral men will proceed all the way to intercourse once you allow them certain privileges with your body. Setting a restrictive standard for physical contact early enough in your relationship can prevent either of you from becoming sexually overstimulated.

These guidelines are meant both for you who have never had intercourse and for you who have had sexual experience but have decided to change your pattern of relating to men.

It bears repeating, I am convinced, that avoiding sex until marriage is the only wise course. In my desire to convince *you* of that fact, I have been greatly encouraged during the past two years. During this time I have had a large and ever-growing number of patients who are virgins or who have stopped having intercourse and plan not to resume sexual activity until marriage.

I know these women are going to experience happier and healthier lives than they would have otherwise. I am excited about this trend because I also believe that these women will gradually convince men that sex is safest and best enjoyed in marriage. There is reason to hope that these women will raise a new generation with values that foster self-confidence about their sexuality. There should then be much less conflict about choosing to keep sex for marriage than exists among the single people of today.

I think this trend points to a new enlightenment whereby people are allowing their morality and their faith to direct them, instead of blindly responding to their physical urges and the pressuring of so-called friends.

Perhaps in the 1990s we will not only see new political freedom burst forth all over the world, but we will also see authentic sexual freedom reign in people's lives as they seek and find the joy of sex in marriage alone.

PART TWO

# STD—
# Symptoms and
# Treatments

# STD Infections
## 1991 Update

| | |
|---|---|
| *Chlamydia* | 3–5 million infections per year.<br>Infects 20–40 percent of sexually active singles. |
| *Human Papillomavirus* | 1.5 million new cases each year in USA.<br>Infects up to 46 percent of sexually active singles. |
| *Herpes* | 500,000 new cases reported each year (low because physicians usually do not report cases).<br>Infects up to 30–40 percent of sexually active singles.<br>20 million Americans are infected. |
| *AIDS* | 1 million new HIV infections in USA in 1990.<br>1 in 100 students at one major university HIV infected. |
| *PID (Pelvic Inflammatory Disease)* | 1 million new cases each year.<br>The most common serious complication of STD because it can result in sterility, hysterectomy, ectopic pregnancies, death. |
| *Gonorrhea* | 1.4 million new infections each year.<br>Antibiotic resistant forms increasing. |
| *Syphilis* | 130,000 new cases each year; infects newborns.<br>Now at 40-year high. |
| *Hepatitis B* | 300,000 new cases each year; infects newborns. |
| *Vaginosis* | Foul-smelling vaginal infection.<br>Millions infected each year.<br>Causes premature deliveries. |
| *Trichomonas* | 3 million new infections each year.<br>Especially aggravating vaginal infection. Frequent cause of liver cancer. Worldwide may be the most common STD. |
| *Urethritis* | Infection of both male and female urinary tract, caused by chlamydia, gonorrhea, and other germs.<br>1.2 million new infections each year. |

These figures were supplied by the Centers for Disease Control, the Journal of the American Medical Association, and from *Chlamydia Infections* published by the American College of OB/GYN.

# 8

# Chlamydia

ONE OF MY patients a few years ago was a high-school student who had become the girlfriend of a "big man on campus" at their school. Soon after they began having intercourse the girl developed some growths on her vulvar area and was having abdominal pain. She saw her family doctor, who treated her venereal warts and gave her antibiotics for the pain. The pain did not subside so he treated her periodically for a year. Still this pain persisted, so he referred this young woman to me for a consultation.

Her doctor had been correct in treating her for pelvic inflammatory disease, but he had been treating the infection as though it were caused by gonorrhea. I identified chlamydia as the culprit and after I treated her with appropriate antibiotics, the abdominal pain finally went away. After her last visit, she was free of both the warts and the pain.

The saddest part of this case history is that, though the infection is gone, this young woman most likely now has serious scarring of her fallopian tubes and ovaries. The scars and adhesions will probably cause infertility in the future unless she undergoes in vitro fertilization or some other costly and difficult fertility procedure. What a terrible expense and heartache for this young woman to anticipate!

## What Is Chlamydia?

Chlamydia is an infection caused by the most common sexually transmitted microorganism in the United States. Contracted only by intercourse, its primary site of infection is a woman's uterus, tubes, and ovaries. This can cause sterility and/or abdominal pain. A woman can receive the infectious organism—*Chlamydia trachomatis*—from a man during intercourse and carry it in her reproductive organs for months and not know it. When the organism starts multiplying in her uterus, tubes, and ovaries, it causes an infection of the pelvic structures called PID (pelvic inflammatory disease). If a woman's reproductive organs have been infected by chlamydia even one time, she has a 25 percent chance of becoming sterile. If she becomes infected a second time, she has a 50 percent chance of sterility. After four such infections, a woman has almost a 100 percent chance of being sterile for the rest of her life unless she has surgery for her infertility problems or has in vitro fertilization, and these are not always successful.

Unfortunately, the misery does not end there. Women whose tubes have only partial scarring may conceive but have a tubal pregnancy. If you have this type of scarring, you have a six times greater chance of having a tubal pregnancy than a woman who has not had a chlamydia (or gonorrhea) infection of her fallopian tubes. Tubal (ectopic) pregnancies can be dangerous. They are the leading cause of death in pregnant women. A tubal pregnancy is a pregnancy that grows in a fallopian tube instead of the uterus. After only three or four weeks the tube is too small to hold the pregnancy and often ruptures, causing hemorrhage inside a woman's abdomen.

It is estimated that over four million people in the United States develop a new chlamydia infection each year. This number may mean more to you if it is broken down into age groups. It is estimated that 8 to 25 percent of all college students are infected with chlamydia. Adolescents have two to three times more chlamydia than adults. The sad conclusion is that it is mainly young people—who have not yet had children—who are unwittingly causing themselves to become sterile. Even more dramatic are studies reporting that 40 percent of sexually active single women are found to have blood tests that show antibodies to chlamydia, indicating either current or previous infection with the organisms. Cultures are positive for chlamydia in up to 19 percent of women examined in general gynecologic clinics, but up to 31 percent of patients in venereal disease treatment centers. It is obvious that chlamydia is a common STD in the United States.

## What Is the Course of a Chlamydia Infection?

When a woman has intercourse with someone who is harboring *Chlamydia trachomatis*, she usually becomes infected with that organism immediately but may not know it for some time. As a matter of fact, 70 percent of people who have this infection are unaware of it. The organism may remain silent in a woman's reproductive organs for a few days or for years. When the organism begins to multiply, it can produce an active infection with a variety of symptoms. An infected woman may experience urethral discharge, burning with urination, an urgency or frequency of urination, and pain in the lower abdomen, just above the pubic bone. She may not have a vaginal discharge, but a doctor's examination may reveal a discharge that looks like infected mucus on her cervix.

If the infection involves her vagina, uterus, tubes, and ovaries, the woman may first notice vaginal discharge (from vaginal and cervical infections). Then, as the infection ascends into the uterus, tubes, and ovaries (PID), low abdominal pain and fever develop. This is the type of infection that can cause later problems with tubal pregnancies and sterility. As a matter of fact, chlamydia is twice as threatening to the fallopian tubes as gonorrhea (with chlamydia, one infection will cause 25 percent of women to be sterile, whereas one infection with gonorrhea will result in sterility in only about 12 to 13 percent of women).

If a chlamydia-related PID is not treated or if the patient does not respond to proper treatment, she may develop pus pockets (abscesses) that may necessitate removal of her uterus, tubes, and ovaries. It is even possible for such a severe pelvic infection to cause death. Untreated, a rampant infection can also spead over the surface of the liver and cause scarring and adhesions of that organ.

In addition to the other problems, chlamydia has been associated with miscarriages, although its exact role is unclear. Finally, if a woman has been infected in the rectum through anal intercourse, she can develop rectal discharge, diarrhea, and rectal pain. These symptoms develop from chlamydia-related ulcerations of the rectum.

Some studies show that from 2 to 37 percent of all women who give birth each year in the United States have chlamydia infections. If a woman has *Chlamydia trachomatis* in her reproductive organs at the time of delivery, she has a six times greater than normal chance of developing a postpartum uterine infection.

Men who become infected with chlamydia often have no symptoms. As many as 70 percent of all infected men will not even know they have the organism present in the urethra. If there are symptoms, they might include a discharge of pus from the penis and burning with urination. A man can also develop epididymitis, which is the most important complication of chlamydia urethritis in males. This condition develops as the infection spreads from the urethra into the epididymis (tube in which sperm from the testis is collected). If not treated properly, it can lead to sterility. A more unusual complication in males is Reiter's syndrome, although the exact relationship between chlamydia and this set of symptoms is not understood completely. Reiter's syndrome is a painful systemic illness, manifested by urethral discharge and burning on urination, irritated eyes (conjunctivitis), and arthritis. Since it is known that patients with Reiter's syndrome have a 50 percent chance of being urethral carriers of chlamydia, any man with Reiter's syndrome should be tested and treated for chlamydia, as should his sexual partners.

Male homosexuals can develop rectal chlamydia infections. Also, having oral sex with an infected person can result in a throat inflammation.

## Can I Have a Chlamydia Infection Without Knowing It?

Yes, you can be unaware that you have chlamydia. You can carry the chlamydia organisms in your genital organs and not have a flare-up of symptoms for days or even years. Most studies say that 70 percent of the people infected with chlamydia have no symptoms. Of course, this means that the disease can be transmitted during intercourse without either partner knowing it. This accounts for the very high incidence of chlamydia in our country. One symptomless chlamydia victim can unknowingly pass the infection to a sexual partner. If he or she also develops no symptoms, the silent cycle of infection continues unchecked.

A much more scary fact for a woman is that she can have chlamydia without the fever or pain that might warn her of a pelvic infection and yet have an infection that can cause her to become sterile or increase her chances of having an ectopic pregnancy later on in life.

I have had a number of infertility patients who for years had been unable to become pregnant. During my evaluation I found some of them to have scars on their fallopian tubes. Asking them about their past history often reveals that although they did have sex with another man before they were married, they never had any signs or symptoms of pelvic infection. The scars and adhesions of their pelvic organs were undoubtedly caused by a very quiet chlamydia infection that occurred years before.

## Can My Partner Have Chlamydia Without My Knowing It?

Yes, of course, as explained in the previous section. Remember, too, that it is possible for a man to have a mild discharge from his penis and not consider this a sign of a sexually transmitted disease. It is also possible that a man can know that he has been exposed to a person with chlamydia but refrains from telling a new sex partner about that exposure. It is fairly common for a man to conveniently "forget" to admit his exposure to an STD for fear that a new partner will then refuse to have intercourse (as well she should!).

## How Is Chlamydia Diagnosed?

If you feel that you might have been exposed to chlamydia and/or if you have any suspicious symptoms, your doctor would probably do a culture of your cervical secretions. Now there are new and relatively inexpensive tests for chlamydia. One is an enzyme-linked immunosorbent assay test (which gives results in 24 hours), and a second is a fluorescent monoclonal antibody test (which gives results in 30 minutes). Both these tests are much less expensive than a chlamydia culture, but they are also less sensitive and can be wrong. The doctor may recommend that a culture of your secretions also be made, but will probably immediately proceed with treating you and your sexual partner if one of the other two tests indicates the presence of chlamydia.

## How Is Chlamydia Treated?

The one uncomplicated aspect of chlamydia is the treatment. A simple infection responds to tetracycline, a drug that most people can take. The usual dosage is 500 mg of tetracycline by mouth, four times a day for seven days; or 100 mg of doxycycline by mouth, twice a day for seven days; or 500 mg of erythromycin by mouth, four times a day for seven days. If a woman is being treated for chlamydia, her sexual partner must also be treated, even if he has no symptoms. If he is not treated he can reinfect her as soon as she stops antibiotics.

The treatment for a woman who has developed PID is much more intense and would depend on how severe the PID was when treatment was begun. It is most important that you see a doctor immediately if you think you have pelvic inflammatory disease, so you can start appropriate treatment quickly.

A person who has chlamydia frequently also has gonorrhea. Many doctors will often treat a patient for both gonorrhea and chlamydia if they have PID. To date, there has not been any resistance to the antibiotic treatment of chlamydia.

## What Are the Dangers of Chlamydia for a Woman?

We have already discussed the primary danger—the risk of becoming sterile. Scarring of a woman's fallopian tubes is the cause of a married couple's infertility in up to 20 to 30 percent of couples and infection with chlamydia is the culprit in at least 50 percent of infertile couples. In fact, the most rapidly increasing cause of infertility in this country is infection and scarring of fallopian tubes from gonorrhea and chlamydia. In addition, as already mentioned, a woman who has this type of infection and scarring may have a greatly increased risk of having a tubal pregnancy. This has produced a three-fold increase in the total number of ectopic pregnancies in the United States during the past twenty years.

During pregnancy, chlamydia is not usually a danger, but a woman with an untreated chlamydia infection has a much greater risk of developing a uterine infection during the first few days after delivery. A baby, however, has about a 66 percent chance of becoming infected during the birth process if the mother has chlamydia. There are three primary dangers for babies from this type of infection. First, they can develop eye infections, which will usually show up five to fourteen days after delivery. This "inclusion conjunctivitis" is usually not a dangerous infection for an infant, even if it is not treated, but it is upsetting to see pus running out of your child's eyes. This infection is treatable with antibiotic cream or drops or with oral antibiotics taken as a syrup.

A second infection that can occur in a baby born to a mother who has chlamydia is a chlamydia pneumonia, which occurs in 10 to 20 percent of babies whose mothers had chlamydia at the time of delivery. It is responsible for 20 to 60 percent of all pneumonia that occurs in the first six months of life. Chlamydia pneumonia usually occurs during the second or third month of life. As with conjunctivitis, this infection is usually not dangerous, but the symptoms—constant coughing, wheezing, and congestion—are disturbing to child and mother. The infection can usually be cleared within a week with antibiotics. If not treated, it can last for months.

A third type of chlamydia-related infection that can occur in babies and very young children affects the middle ear (otitis media). One study showed that 60 percent of infants with chlamydial pneumonia had middle ear infections, and the chlamydia organism could be cultured out of the material from many of those children's ears.

## Implications

Listed below are the important facts to remember about chlamydia:

1. Chlamydia is often a silent infection, and up to 80 percent of people who have it are not aware of it.

2. Chlamydia is an extremely common sexually transmitted infection. In some groups of young men and women, as many as 20 to 40 percent are infected.

3. It is a devastating infection for a woman. There is evidence that it can cause miscarriages or premature births. It is a major cause of tubal pregnancies, which are medically dangerous and emotionally painful. The most devastating thing about chlamydia for a woman is that it can develop into PID, which may cause sterility that can lead to years of expense and heartache.

4. If a pregnant woman has chlamydia at the time of delivery, her baby may develop an eye infection, pneumonia, and/or a middle ear infection.

5. A woman who has chlamydia will often have another sexually transmitted disease. It is important that she be tested for other STDs as soon as the chlamydia is diagnosed.

6. Although men can develop epididymitis or sterility from chlamydia, this is not very common. This disease primarily ravages women. An article in the *Journal of the American Medical Association* (April 17, 1987) estimated the basic cost of chlamydia for a man as $50. If he needs to be hospitalized, the average cost would be $1,876. For women, the cost of a simple chlamydia infection would be about $150. Hospitalization, if needed, would cost $3,421; an ectopic pregnancy, $4,235; and an infertility evaluation, $2,500. In addition, there may be long-term expenses in an effort to reverse chlamydia-related sterility that run into many thousands of dollars—and may sometimes be fruitless. The point is that this is an extremely expensive and devastating infection for a woman, yet it is avoidable!

# 9

# Herpes

ANN IS FORTY years old. She recently came to my office for her annual examination. As we talked about her health, she told me she thought that cortisone injections for a chronic health problem were causing painful sores on her vulva. Ann suspected that these ulcers were herpes. She was correct.

Ann had probably been infected with herpes during a long-ago sexual relationship. Most of the time, the herpes virus she carries has caused no problems. Now, however, the painful sores that were brought on by the necessary cortisone shots were so bad that she would need to take daily Zovirax medication to prevent the outbreaks.

Ann can take Zovirax for only one year, the maximum continuous limit set by the FDA. Then Ann will probably suffer herpes outbreaks again and can take Zovirax for another year. The bottom line for Ann is that she must spend a great deal of money and time taking an anti-viral medication three or four times a day merely to *control* the symptoms of a sexually transmitted disease she contracted when she was much younger.

As Ann learned the hard way, herpes is a maddening disease. It is incurable, and while it is usually controllable, bothersome outbreaks can occur at the most inopportune times and for a variety of reasons.

## What Is Herpes?

Herpes is caused by a virus that produces blisters and sores in and on the sex organs. In men, the blisters may appear on the penis, the scrotum, or the anus; in women, the sores may be on the vulva, inside the vagina, on the cervix, or in the anal region. In both men and women, the outbreaks may also occur on the skin, anywhere on the body.

The infective virus, *herpes simplex type II*, is spread by direct contact with someone who carries it. This contact may be sexual intercourse, but the virus can be spread by mouth, so herpes sores on the lips may result from kissing or from oral-genital contact with an infected individual.

The herpes virus does not remain in the area where initial contact is made. It invades the body and finally lodges in groups of nerve cells (ganglia) located near the spinal cord. When it is causing its typical sores, the virus spreads through the nerves to the genitals or the skin. For this reason, merely treating the area of the sores will not prevent a future herpes outbreak.

There are two other related diseases. One is the common fever blister or "cold sore." This is caused by the virus *herpes simplex type I.*

There is also a disease called herpes zoster, commonly referred to as "shingles." However, it is not caused by either one of the herpes viruses, so its diagnosis and care are totally unrelated to that for herpes I or II.

## What Is the Course of Herpes Infection?

Once the herpes virus gets into the tissues, it is probably there to stay. The initial outbreak may not occur for two weeks, several months, or even several years after the first contact! Even if it *never* causes an outbreak, the person carrying the virus is infectious. When the first herpes outbreak does occur, it is usually much more severe than later recurrences.

Herpes blisters are often extremely painful. Before the blisters develop, there may be local pain, tingling, itching, or burning. After the blisters form, they usually break open, leaving small, superficial sores that may vary from as small as an eighth of an inch to more than an inch across. The first herpes outbreak in a woman can be so painful that she is unable to urinate. Women with this much discomfort may have to be admitted to a hospital for catheterization and medication.

If the first outbreak of herpes is not treated, the duration of the ulcers will be longer, often taking two to four weeks to heal. About 50 percent of those who have an initial herpes outbreak of this type never have a recurrence. For the other 50 percent, recurrences may be only once a year (or even less frequently). Or new outbreaks may occur several times a year or several times a month. Women often find that their menstrual periods bring on a herpes attack. Intercourse, stress, tight clothes, and other factors (as with Ann's cortisone shots) can also cause recurrences.

An outbreak of herpes can cause enlarged lymph nodes in the groin. Flu-like symptoms may occur in the form of fever and muscle aches. These symptoms usually appear only with the first—and worst—episode of the herpes infection.

## Can I Have Herpes Without Knowing It?

Unfortunately, yes. It is not unusual to have herpes without knowing it. An article in the *Dallas Times Herald* (July 20, 1986), quoted Dr. Mary Guinan, associate director of the Division of Sexually Transmitted Disease, U.S. Centers for Disease Control in Atlanta, as saying that 23 percent of

American adults have been infected with genital herpes, but only about 25 percent of those have symptoms. A more recent report shows that herpes may now be even more widespread. Yvonne Bryson, M.S., associate professor of pediatrics of the University of California, Los Angeles, School of Medicine, reported in the *American Medical Association News* (June 2, 1989) that "in L.A., Seattle and Atlanta—25% to 60% of women tested were positive for the type II infection." Robert E. Johnson and his associates reported in the *New England Journal of Medicine* (July 6, 1989, vol. 321, no. 1) their conclusion that "the prevalence of HSV-2 (herpes 2) infection in the United States is higher than has previously been recognized." Such studies validate the conclusion that the disease can be spread even when there are no symptoms.

The *OB-GYN News* of May 1–14, 1987, reported that about 50 to 70 percent of neonatal herpes occurs in infants whose mothers have no history of genital herpes. This means that a baby may contract herpes during birth though the mother was unaware that she had been infected. (This was reported by Dr. Lisa Frenkel of the University of California, Los Angeles, School of Medicine.) Even if there have never been symptoms, you may be carrying the virus and could pass it on to someone in the future.

## Can My Partner Have Herpes Without My Knowing It?

Yes. Anyone can have herpes and be unaware of it. Even if your partner knows about his infection, he might be dishonest with you and conceal his past outbreaks. People who know they have herpes often feel "safe" in having sex if they do not at that moment have an outbreak. Remember, though, that the virus can be spread even though symptoms are not present at the time of intercourse. Not only does the herpes virus "shed" a few hours before the actual outbreak (and continue to shed for a while *after* the outbreak has subsided), but also herpes sores can be so small and painless that an outbreak is barely noticeable and therefore considered unimportant. In addition, apparently normal skin and vaginal lining in a herpes-infected individual can shed the virus even though there have *never* been any sores.

## How Is Herpes Diagnosed?

If you have sex with a man who has herpes and become infected, you will probably have an initial outbreak from two days to two weeks after the exposure. An experienced doctor may be able to tell by looking at a blister whether or not it is herpes. Although I am able to make a fairly accurate diagnosis this way, I never tell a patient for sure that she has herpes without doing a culture to confirm my opinion. The doctor will swab the ulcer to obtain secretions to send to the laboratory. If the culture proves positive, herpes is present; if it is negative, the patient may or may not have herpes, since the culture results can be wrong up to 15 or 20 percent of the time. The culture might be repeated if another outbreak occurs, but—if the outbreak is in the same spot and appears typical of herpes—a culture is hardly necessary. Continued outbreaks almost certainly mean herpes.

The herpes culture procedure is expensive. Somewhat less costly tests can be done, but they are less accurate. A blood test will show whether or not you have ever been infected with the herpes virus, but it is not useful in determining whether you have contracted herpes recently unless you know for certain that your blood was herpes negative in the past. (I almost never order this type of blood test.)

## How Is Herpes Treated?

Herpes outbreaks sometimes stop without treatment. Remember, there is no medical cure for *any virus,* including herpes and the common cold. But there are differences in how various viruses affect humans. The difference between the cold virus and the herpes virus is that the cold virus must be *re-caught* to produce another infection; the herpes virus is caught once and its effects keep coming back for years.

For an outbreak of herpes, whether involving fever-blisters or genital sores, Zovirax ointment can be applied to the sores every three hours. With this treatment, the sores will be less painful and disappear more quickly than otherwise.

For recurrent outbreaks of herpes, Zovirax capsules (200 mg) can be taken from one to three times a day for up to one year. (Longer usage has not been approved.) With this long-term use, 40 to 75 percent of herpes sufferers will have very few recurrences (or none) during the time they take the medication. After completing a one-year course, it is recommended that the person stop the medication. If outbreaks occur again, it seems safe to restart Zovirax for another year. It seems to be a relatively safe drug, but it is obtained only by prescription and is expensive.

## Is Herpes Dangerous?

Although herpes is inconvenient and uncomfortable, there is very little medical danger from the infection unless a person has an impaired immune system due to, for example, chemotherapy or AIDS. Herpes does not cause cancer and it almost never permanently injures a person's body. It is usually no more damaging to the body than the fever blisters many people get. However, if herpes virus, either type I or II, infects a person's eyes, it can cause serious scarring, although that type of infection is rare. Very rarely herpes encephalitis can result from a herpes infection.

Discomfort from herpes can be extreme, especially with the first outbreak. When treated with Zovirax, the initial outbreak usually does not last  long, and the time during which a person cannot urinate normally or is uncomfortable is fairly short.

The most severe and widespread effect of herpes is its emotional impact. An article by Noel Gallagher in *Mother Jones Magazine* (1982) elaborates:

> If you listen to what herpes victims say, the overriding feelings they have are anger and guilt. Part of the anger is

due to having an incurable disease in an age when almost anything can be fixed and, once fixed, forgotten. Guilt arises because it is currently fashionable to place some blame on the patient for getting sick. Add to that a disease that comes and goes of its own free will, and you get a feeling of helplessness.

There is also the worry of being contagious. It is hard to convey how terrible some herpes sufferers feel about carrying around a disease. They feel, they say, like lepers. They feel "disgusting, sleazy" and the feelings are compounded if the person gives the virus to someone else.

According to the Herpes Resource Center [herpes victims] are usually well-educated, middle to upper class. They are used to having a lot of control over their lives. They are used to being healthy. Herpes directly attacks their sense of control.

Finally, there is the sexual guilt, perhaps the most pervasive of all herpes symptoms. "I felt I deserved it," said Linda, "because I picked it up while going through a promiscuous stage." This guilt is reinforced by the overreactions of others. Linda's roommate used to scrub out the bathtub with Comet after Linda used it and before she herself stepped in.

Herpes *has* been associated with an increased risk of miscarriage or premature delivery, and an increased risk of delivering babies with a low birth weight (which sometimes means that these babies have not developed properly in their mother's uterus).

While these effects of herpes have not been absolutely proven, it is true that if a baby is born to a woman with herpes virus, the baby may be infected by the mother. About 65 percent of herpes-infected babies will die, and only 10 percent of those who survive will be normal. (The rest will develop damage to their brains and central nervous systems.) Even if a baby's herpes infection is treated with Zovirax, its chance of dying is decreased only slightly, and damage to the brain may still occur.

Fortunately, most infants who are born to mothers with herpes, even to those with an active herpes infection, will not become infected. Of approximately four million babies born in the United States every year, only about one hundred are born with herpes.

## Implications

Herpes is a *sexually* transmitted disease that is almost always contracted through intercourse or other intimate physical contact. The only way it can be caught from a toilet seat is by coming in direct contact with infectious secretions that have *very recently* been left on the seat by someone else. You also do not need to worry about catching this disease by shaking hands or hugging or similar contact with others. Herpes can be contracted by kissing.

Herpes is very prevalent as the studies already cited have shown. Remember that 75 percent of herpes-infected individuals have never had an outbreak of herpes (and therefore may be unaware of its existence) but can pass it on nevertheless.

Dr. Andre Nahmias, of Emory University School of Medicine in Atlanta, reported in the *Journal of the American Medical Association* (April 4, 1986) a study suggesting that 20 to 60 percent of our population has genital herpes, and that the average male adult in the United States has almost a 50 percent chance of having already been infected with the virus.

The bad news about herpes is that it can be painful, embarrassing, terribly annoying, and expensive—and places an unborn baby at risk if the mother is infected. Somewhat better news is that it is not a dangerous disease, except to very few people. In fact, after four or five years, some people may actually stop having recurrences of herpes outbreaks. The best news is that you never have to worry about this problem if you take the advice outlined in Part One.

# Gonorrhea

Dr. Herman L. Gardner, in the book *Benign Diseases of the Vulva and Vagina*, which he coauthored with Raymond Kaufman, states, "Gonorrhea is probably the most important bacterial infection to the civilized world. It has plagued kings and slaves alike since the days of Aristotle."

## What Is Gonorrhea?

Gonorrhea is a sexually transmitted disease caused by the gonococcus *(Neisseria gonorrhoeae)*, a pus-producing bacterium that is almost never transmitted any other way than by intercourse. Although gonorrhea is often thought to be a disease of the past, the threat from gonorrhea is still very real and is growing. Gonorrhea is highly communicable—even a one-time sexual act with an infected partner brings a 40 percent chance of contracting this disease.

The incidence of gonorrhea is increasing dramatically in the United States. Drs. Gardner and Kaufman state that the number of gonorrhea cases in the United States has been steadily rising since 1958 and has nearly doubled since 1965.

Their book was published in 1981, and since then the number of people with gonorrhea has risen even more dramatically.

One of the main problems with gonorrhea, as with certain other STDs, is that it can be present and produce absolutely no noticeable symptoms. This fact alone makes gonorrhea, along with chlamydia, dangerous.

## What Is the Course of Gonorrhea Infection?

A woman who has contracted gonorrhea from intercourse with a man who has the disease may have symptoms within days or within a few months. Even if there are no symptoms, she can carry the gonococci during this time and be able to transmit it. The infection may involve only her vulva, urethra, bladder, vagina, and cervix—or it can extend to her uterus, tubes, and ovaries. Early symptoms may include burning with urination and a pus-like discharge from the urethra. Although the infection may cause the need to urinate frequently, it may also make urination painful or impossible. In this case, catheterization is necessary.

If the Bartholin's glands, which provide secretions and moisture for a woman's vulva, become infected, the glands can swell, become abscessed, or develop cysts. Surgery may then be required, and gynecologists frequently see this problem. An affected gland can continue to be cystic and painful for years, long after the gonorrhea organism has been treated and eradicated.

Gonorrhea can also cause a vaginal discharge due to infection of the walls of the vagina, the cervix, the uterus, tubes, and/or ovaries. If gonorrhea invades a woman's uterus, tubes, and ovaries (PID, or pelvic inflammatory disease), it often causes the fallopian tubes to become closed. The pelvic organs—tubes, ovaries, uterus and intestines—may stick together as though glue has been poured over them. The disease can create pockets of pus (abscesses). This type of infection is the most rapidly increasing cause of infertility in our society.

A man who becomes infected with gonorrhea may not notice any problem for some time. When there are symptoms, early signs of trouble may be burning on urination and the need to urinate frequently. Further symptoms may include a fairly heavy, pus-like discharge from the penis.

Although all the above symptoms usually develop sometime during the course of a man's infection with gonorrhea, he *may* be carrying the disease for a long time without them. In that case, he will be unaware that he has a disease that is transmissible through intercourse.

Both men and women can develop rectal infections from gonorrhea if they have anal intercourse. This causes symptoms of diarrhea, pus in the stool, painful bowel movements, and irritation of the anus.

Gonorrhea-infected men and women who engage in oral sex may spread the infection to the mouth and throat (gonorrhea pharyngitis). Other possible complications of a gonorrhea infection include high fever, skin rash, and even arthritis. Hospitalization may be required at that point.

## Can I Have Gonorrhea Without Knowing It?

As with many other sexually transmitted diseases, a person can carry the gonorrhea organism without being aware of its presence. Even so, the infectious agent can be passed to a sexual partner. It is estimated that 80 percent of women infected with gonorrhea do not know about it in the early stages.

## Can My Sexual Partner Have Gonorrhea Without My Knowing It?

Men, too, can have gonorrhea and be unaware of its existence. About 80 percent of *both* men and women who have gonorrhea have no knowledge of it for varying lengths of time. As mentioned, the disease can be transmitted from one person to another during this symptomless period.

## How Is Gonorrhea Diagnosed?

If gonorrhea is suspected, the secretions from a man's penis or from a woman's cervix or vagina are cultured. If gonococci grow, the diagnosis of gonorrhea is made. At the same time, the doctor may want to culture the patient for chlamydia. This is because 20 to 40 percent of those who have gonorrhea also have chlamydia, but the treatments for the two infections are not necessarily alike. If both diseases are present, a patient usually would need two different antibiotics instead of one.

## How Is Gonorrhea Treated?

Most uncomplicated gonorrhea responds to treatment with penicillin, ampicillin, or tetracycline—three common antibiotics. If chlamydia is also present, two antibiotics are usually prescribed because gonorrhea responds best to penicillin-like antibiotics and chlamydia responds best to tetracycline [see chapter 8].

One of the issues about this disease that is of concern is that a strain of gonococci resistant to penicillin has been found in all fifty states. Because of this, a drug called ceftriaxone (Rocephin) or one of the newer cephalosporin antibiotics is now being recommended for the treatment of gonorrhea. These antibiotics may cost about ten times as much as penicillin, the more traditional drug. Unfortunately, it has recently been found that some gonorrhea strains are resistant to even these newer antibiotics.

When a woman whose infection of the fallopian tubes is caused by resistant gonococci is treated with penicillin, the infection will continue to damage her tubes until an effective antibiotic is given. By that time, she may be irreversibly sterile.

If a woman develops a generalized pelvic infection (PID) from gonorrhea, she will require much more intensive antibiotic treatment. Hospitalization may also be necessary.

## What Are the Dangers of Gonorrhea?

The most dangerous thing about gonorrhea is that many people take the infection lightly and feel that it is not a special threat to them.

Men do not ordinarily have many problems from a gonorrhea infection, unless it is untreated. In that case, the disease can cause scarring and abnormalities of the urethra.

On the other hand, a woman can develop significant medical problems, even if the disease is treated. For example, a Bartholin's gland infection may require surgery and continue to recur for many years.

If a woman develops PID, she can become sterile. To a young, unmarried woman, PID may not seem too much of a problem at the time. When this woman marries, however, and is ready to start her family, the sterility caused by a long-forgotten gonorrhea infection may seem the worst tragedy in the world.

The same gonorrhea-related scarring that can cause a woman to be infertile may also cause pelvic pain month after month, and the pain can be aggravated by every act of intercourse. This kind of chronic pain, or continued infection that does not respond to antibiotics, can eventually necessitate a hysterectomy, with removal of not only the uterus but also the tubes and ovaries. Infertility, painful intercourse, or premature hysterectomy usually brings great sorrow to a woman's life.

The above discussion reminds me of a young married patient who was rushed to our office with pain from PID. Her emergency surgery required the removal of her uterus, tubes, and ovaries. Laboratory cultures confirmed that the infection was caused by gonorrhea transmitted by her husband, who had recently had an affair. They are now divorced, but this wonderful woman will never have the large family she had wanted.

Even if sterility does not result from the gonorrhea, subtle damage to the fallopian tubes can cause a much higher chance of tubal pregnancy. A woman who has had a gonorrhea or chlamydia infection has a six times greater chance of having an ectopic pregnancy than one who has never had either disease.

Dr. Lane J. Mercer, in a speech given recently in Chicago, stated that PID is the major cause of hospitalization for reproductive age women. He added that one in seven couples trying to achieve pregnancy is infertile, often because the woman has blocked fallopian tubes from the PID caused by a sexually transmitted disease.

After one episode of gonorrhea, a woman has about a 12 percent chance of becoming infertile. After a second episode, the chances are 25 percent. This percentage increases dramatically as the number of infections increases.

As far as is currently known, neither a pregnant woman with gonorrhea nor the baby she is carrying will have complications during the pregnancy. The problem comes at delivery. As the baby passes through the birth canal, it picks up the gonorrhea organism, which then can infect the baby's eyes *(Gonococcal ophthalmia neonatorum)* and cause blindness if not treated.

One of the major successes of preventive medicine in our modern medical age was the discovery that 2 percent silver nitrate solution, used to wash a newborn's eyes, prevents this problem. The solution kills any gonococci present, and all newborns in the United States are now routinely treated with this or some antibiotic solution. In developing countries, where medical treatment is not as advanced, gonorrhea is still a major cause of blindness.

## Implications

Although gonorrhea has been around so long that it is sometimes laughingly considered a relic of the past, it is no joke to those who become infected by it. Here are some of the facts concerning this dreadful disease:

1. For women, gonorrhea can cause abscesses of the vulva and Bartholin's gland cysts. The possible long-term effects of a gonorrhea infection include sterility, tubal pregnancies, cystic ovaries, chronic pelvic pain, and need for a hysterectomy. Gonorrhea can also cause blindness in babies who are untreated after delivery.

2. Men who are untreated for gonorrhea may develop scarring of the urethra, which can cause difficult urinary-tract problems.

3. Antibiotic-resistant gonorrhea strains are becoming increasingly common in the United States. While this does not mean that gonorrhea cannot be treated, treatment can now cost ten times as much as it would if the germ were responsive to penicillin. It also means that major damage can be done to the female organs by the time a physician realizes that the germ is a resistant strain.

4. If a woman uses an IUD (intrauterine device to prevent conception), she is from two to four times more likely to develop PID if she becomes infected with gonorrhea.

5. While antibiotics can kill the gonorrhea organisms, they cannot erase the scars that have already resulted from the infection. Complications may remain. If gonorrhea has produced scarring, adhesions, or blocked fallopian tubes, the condition will remain long after the gonococci have been eradicated—and may have permanent effects on a woman's health and/or fertility.

# Syphilis

MARY WAS EMBARRASSED and nervous about going to the campus health clinic to have a small, painless genital sore examined, but she was worried about the lesion. A native of South America, Mary had come to the United States to attend college and had recently been talked into having intercourse by a fellow student.

The health-center doctor was unable to identify the cause of Mary's sore. He excised a sample and sent it to the lab, but the report only showed "inflammation." It was not tested for syphilis.

When the sore did not disappear, the clinic doctor referred Mary to my associate, who was almost certain that Mary had syphilis. Checking a smear of the lesion under a microscope confirmed his diagnosis. It *was* syphilis.

Mary was treated with penicillin and cured of the syphilis. She was very fortunate. Although penicillin is totally effective for syphilis, many men and women either ignore their symptoms or are not aware of them. Others have no symptoms for many years. Untreated, syphilis can eventually result in insanity, fatal blood vessel and bone damage, and many other very serious health problems.

**What Is Syphilis?**

Syphilis is a sexually transmitted disease that results from infection with the syphilis organism, *Treponema pallidum*. This is a spirochete, so named because of its somewhat corkscrew-shaped appearance. The syphilis organism dies quickly if it is not in a warm, moist environment. It can be transmitted only from one moist area to another and it is almost entirely a sexually transmitted disease.

In their previously cited book, *Benign Diseases of the Vulva and Vagina*, Drs. Herman L. Gardner and Raymond Kaufman write:

> Syphilis is a continuous infectious process that is initiated at the time of contact. It passes through well-known clinical stages: incubation, primary, secondary, latent, and late (tertiary). Transmission of syphilis involves intimacy, and in the vast majority of cases, it is attributable to sexual contact.
>
> Many recorded examples have occurred from kissing. Spirochetes (the syphilis organism) readily invade intact, moist mucus membranes. Invasion through dry, unbroken skin is unlikely.
>
> According to estimates, approximately half of the patients with syphilis are either unaware of its presence, or consider the lesions inconsequential until the disease is past its early stages.
>
> Although the patient is actually infected from the moment of inoculation (the time of intercourse from which he or she gets the infections), the primary lesions (chancres) usually do not appear for ten to ninety days, the average being three weeks. Serologic (blood) tests do not become positive for an additional week or longer.

**What Is the Course of Syphilis Infection?**

During intimate sexual contact, spirochetes from the moist tissues of a syphilis-infected person can be transmitted to the moist tissues of the sexual partner. Within a few days or weeks of having sex with a man who has syphilis, about 50 percent of women will become infected. In the initial stage of syphilis, a chancre will develop at the place where the organism invaded the body. These sores may appear on the vulva, in the vagina (or on the penis), in the mouth, or on the lips. It is common for a woman to have more than one chancre with a first syphilis infection.

A chancre often starts as an ulcer but later becomes a knot, with a punched-out, thickened base and firm, rolled edges. (Some chancres may remain soft, however.) The lesions are usually from one-half inch to one inch across. The most typical characteristic of a syphilitic chancre is that it is painless. Because there is no pain, many people ignore these seemingly insignificant sores.

Secondary syphilis develops from six weeks to six months after the initial infection. This second stage is when the disease is most infectious. Symptoms may include headache, fatigue, low-grade fever, skin rash, and enlarged lymph nodes.

In addition, *Condylomae lata* (raised growths, which are flat-topped, moist, and gray in color) may develop on the skin. The growths may become ulcerated and thickened and may ooze some fluid. These condylome, which may appear in the mouth, beneath the breasts, and under the arms, teem with spirochetes, and are extremely infectious. Enlargement of the lymph nodes in the groin usually accompanies the appearance of *Condylomae lata*.

The episode of secondary syphilis will pass, even without treatment. At that time the signs of syphilis will disappear spontaneously, and a latent period will follow, lasting from several months to twenty years. During the latent period, there are essentially no outward symptoms of syphilis, and the disease is relatively noncontagious.

When syphilis reaches the late stage, it can produce devastating medical problems in almost any part of the body. Some of the more common effects are aneurysms of the cardiovascular system, deterioration of the central nervous system, involvement of bones, and damage to peripheral nerves.

## Can I Have Syphilis Without Knowing It?

A woman will usually develop a chancre during the initial stage of syphilis. But since it can be high inside her vagina, she might be totally unaware of its presence. Because of this—and the fact that even a visible lesion is painless—she will usually not realize that she has been infected.

A man will usually be more aware of the initial stage, because he will have a noticeable chancre on his penis or scrotum or on his lips. Any such chancres should, of course, be evaluated by a doctor who is told that there is a possibility of sexually transmitted disease. Physicians see so few patients with syphilis these days that it is easy to misdiagnose the symptoms (just as the doctor at the student health center failed to identify Mary's syphilis).

Generally, both men and women are aware of secondary syphilis. The skin changes and/or growths are usually obvious, but doctors may not recognize them as syphilis.

Once syphilis becomes latent, however, there is no evidence of its presence, except a blood test which is positive for syphilis. In spite of the fact that there are no symptoms during this phase, the disease process is insidiously working in the body. Eventually, perhaps as long as twenty years later, this process can result in insanity, paralysis, fatal damage to blood vessels, and severe bone deterioration.

## Can My Sexual Partner Have Syphilis Without My Knowing It?

As with many other sexually transmitted diseases, there are often no symptoms one would notice about a syphilis-infected partner. A man may not tell you of a painless sore on his genitals because he may not think it is important, even if it is not his intention to deceive you. (The skin growths, which appear in the secondary stage, are usually more noticeable but may be misdiagnosed.)

Again, as with other STDs, there is always the possibility that a man will not tell you about his infection if he believes you would then deny him sex—which you should, of course!

## How Is Syphilis Diagnosed?

When the initial infectious episode of syphilis produces a chancre, which it commonly does, the doctor may microscopically examine a smear of the secretions from the chancre. If it is syphilis, the spirochetes will usually be identifiable. If you or your doctor suspect that you might have syphilis (for whatever reason), he or she would examine you to see if you have any of the physical changes that are typical of a syphilitic infection. Even if you do not, you could still have been infected, so a blood test for syphilis should be done if there is any question. If it is positive, treatment should begin immediately.

If you do not believe you have been exposed to syphilis but are worried about the possibility because you have had intercourse outside of marriage, have a syphilis blood test. Unless you have symptoms, it is advisable to delay testing for six months after the "suspicious" sexual contact. It can take that long for a blood test to register a positive finding.

## How Is Syphilis Treated?

The standard treatment for syphilis is penicillin, a drug that is still 100 percent effective in killing the Treponema that causes the disease. Alternative antibiotics are available for those allergic to penicillin.

If syphilis is not diagnosed and treated, it will be working silent destruction in its victim's body day after day and year after year. Then, even if the disease is recognized and the infection is treated, the damage has already been done. The effects will usually not get worse once the spirochetes are killed, but they will linger. If a syphilitic woman has a baby before she is treated for her infection, syphilis can adversely affect her child during the pregnancy. (See the following segment for more information.) Remember, there are two primary impediments to the early diagnosis of syphilis that you must guard against:

1. You may not have any symptoms when you are first infected. If you suspect that you might have become infected, ask a doctor to examine and test you, as well as the person who might have infected you.

2. The symptoms and signs of syphilis are very confusing, and doctors do not see syphilis very often. Thus, a doctor might not immediately diagnose your syphilis. Again, if you suspect that you might have been exposed to syphilis, have your doctor examine and test both you and the suspected partner. Insist on repeated tests or another opinion if you are still in doubt.

## What Are the Dangers of Syphilis?

The first two stages of syphilis present no serious danger to your body, in and of themselves. The danger lies in ignoring the disease until its latent stage, although if you are pregnant, there *is* great danger to a baby, even from early syphilis. There is also great risk for an unsuspecting sexual partner during the highly contagious early stages.

During the latent stage, the syphilis spirochetes do tremendous damage throughout the body. Large abscesses are formed and entire organs can be destroyed. Once well into the latent stage, a patient may sustain irreversible damage to the bones, liver cells, heart valves, blood vessels, and central nervous system.

*There is one major threat that occurs during all stages of syphilis—damage to the unborn child of a syphilitic mother.*

Babies can develop syphilis while still in their mother's womb, and congenital syphilis is a disaster. Such pregnancies often end in spontaneous miscarriages or stillbirths. Other infected babies die soon after birth. Those that live are often born with such abnormalities as nose obstruction, flattening of the bridge of the nose, fractures of the bones, enlarged liver and spleen, and eye or ear damage.

*Population Reports* (July 1983) quotes a study showing that of 220 pregnancies in women with untreated primary or secondary syphilis, 38 percent ended in spontaneous miscarriages, stillbirths, or neonatal death; and 41 percent resulted in the birth of a syphilitic infant. By contrast, of 482 women with *latent* syphilis (when the disease is less infectious), 74 percent delivered healthy full-term babies. Of course, 26 percent did have damaged babies.

## Implications

There are many facts about syphilis that are important enough to keep in mind:

1. The incidence of syphilis has recently surged dramatically; for the past few years it has been occurring at the highest rate since 1950. In 1987, syphilis increased 25 percent, and it increased another 25 percent in 1988. Public health officials are alarmed.

2. Syphilis is a sexually transmitted disease passed by intimate sexual contact, including intercourse, kissing, and oral/genital contact.

3. A man in the latent stage of syphilis is not as likely to transmit the disease to a sexual partner as in the primary and secondary stages. *A woman, however, can transmit syphilis during the menstrual period, even in the latent phase.* (Menstrual flow contains the spirochete germ, even in the latent stage.)

4. Approximately 42 percent of people who have intercourse *one time* with a person who has syphilis do not

become infected. This means, however, that over 50 percent *do* (*British Journal of Venereal Disease*, 1983).

5. Even extremely competent doctors can miss the diagnosis of syphilis because it is often difficult to identify *initially*, even when laboratory techniques are used.

6. It is not against the law to have syphilis. Your doctor will not report it to the police but will make a confidential report to your local public health department. This allows them to trace this silent killer and identify people who are infected and don't know it.

7. Syphilis affects women more adversely than it does men. In the last three years of the 1980s, the national incidence of syphilis increased 30 percent, but the increase among women was 60 to 75 percent.

# 12

# Human Papillomavirus (HPV) Infections—Venereal Warts

SINCE MILDRED WAS never at her best meeting new people, consulting a new doctor, and knowing that he was going to do a pelvic exam, was a prospect that absolutely terrified this eighteen-year-old. Mildred was especially worried because her family doctor had diagnosed the growths on her vulva as caused by a sexually transmitted disease. He had suggested she see a specialist.

Barely able to speak through her nervousness and fear, Mildred did manage to give me a general idea of her problem. Even before the examination, I was certain that she had venereal warts, caused by the human papillomavirus (HPV). Mildred felt better when I assured her that the warts could be treated, but her embarrassment and nervousness were painful to see. Happily, a chemical application (podophyllin) eliminated her warts with just one treatment.

Mildred was fortunate. And smart. Coming in for treatment early may have prevented a more difficult, expensive, and lengthy course of treatment. I have seen women delay seeing a doctor until warts as large as a fist were hanging from their vulva.

Meg, another patient, was also fortunate. An annual examination and Pap smear revealed precancerous cells on her cervix—another abnormality caused by the human papillomavirus. Had we not found and treated these cells, they would have developed into cancer. Meg's HPV infection had started with an episode of intercourse she had while she was in college three years before.

It is amazing how few people know about the human papillomavirus, since the disease is so prevalent and causes so much damage. Recent studies have shown that the HPV virus can be found in the tissues of as many as 33 percent of women in the United States.

## What Is HPV Infection?

The virus group causing venereal warts is essentially passed only by sexual intercourse and is therefore a true sexually transmitted disease.

Infection by an HPV can cause growths of soft warts on the genitals. In men, the warts can develop on the penis, on the scrotum, or sometimes (due to anal intercourse) in or around the anus. They can also occur in the groin area. These warts are very contagious. Roughly 85 percent of women whose regular sex partners have these warts will develop similar growths within eight months. In women, the warts may appear in the groin, on the vulva, or (with or without anal intercourse) in or around the anus. They also commonly occur in the vagina and on the cervix.

Venereal warts are only mildly irritating. They do not burn, and usually do not itch. A woman will often be unaware of the warts if they are inside the vagina. I have found, though, that women are often very bothered emotionally to know that they have venereal warts. It is probably not the physical discomfort but the mental concerns that are worrisome.

Physicians and medical science have only in the past few years begun realizing another significant fact about HPV infection. *Essentially all abnormal Pap smears indicating precancerous cells are a result of infection from this sexually transmitted virus.* Studies done recently show that between 63 and 80 percent of the current male partners of women with abnormal (premalignant) Pap smears had venereal warts on their penis. It is primarily because of this sexually transmitted disease that doctors advise every woman to have a Pap smear every year. This is the impact that just one STD has already had in our society.

The human papillomavirus can cause changes of the skin cells of the penis, the vagina, and the vulva that may develop into precancerous growths. Abnormal cells of any of these organs will remain in a precancerous state for a while, but, if untreated, they can eventually change into invasive cancer.

An increasing problem from genital HPV infection is discomfort at the entrance to the vagina. This is called vestibulitis. Symptoms are vulvar irritation, burning, itching, and pain, especially with intercourse. This very distressing problem is difficult both to diagnose and to treat.

If a woman becomes infected with a very aggressive form of this virus, or if she has not had a diagnostic Pap smear for several years, she may develop cancer of the cervix and not know it. The same thing can happen to a woman's vagina or vulva if she does not have regular exams that would discover the abnormalities early enough to treat successfully.

## What Is the Cause of HPV Infection?

HPV infections are caused by a whole group of viruses of which there are over sixty types. (HPV types 6, 11, 16, 18, 31, 33, and 35 are the ones that usually cause venereal warts and cancerous and precancerous changes of the genitals of both men and women, but other HPV types have also been associated with growths or abnormalities on the genitals.) Apparently, when one of these viruses invades the tissues of the penis, vulva, vagina, or cervix, it stimulates abnormal changes in the cells, including an actual altering of the chromosomes. HPV does not normally cause warts on other parts of the body.

### Can I Have an HPV Infection Without Knowing It?

One of the biggest problems with a genital HPV infection is that it can be undetected for so long. Recent studies have shown that 10 percent of otherwise healthy women have the virus in their vagina without developing a wart and without having an abnormal Pap smear. It seems clear that a woman may be exposed to the HPV and neither develop a wart nor show a precancerous or cancerous change on a Pap smear for many months after infection.

### Can My Sexual Partner Have an HPV Infection Without My Knowing It?

Either you or your sexual partner can have an HPV infection without being aware of it. A man may have very small venereal warts on his penis or scrotum without realizing there is anything to worry about. He may dismiss the growth as merely a "blackhead." Furthermore, a man may have this virus in the skin of his penis and not know it because there is no wart. Of course, the possibility of deception is always a factor with any sexually transmitted disease. Your partner may indeed be aware of a small wart and just not tell you about it.

Whether or not a person is aware of the infection, it can still be transmitted to a sexual partner. However, it is not known how long a person can carry the virus—with no warts and other organic changes—and still be able to pass it on to a partner. It seems obvious that the communicable period may last many months.

## How Is an HPV Infection Diagnosed?

When a woman goes to her doctor because of small wart-like genital growths, the doctor will look carefully at them, perhaps with a magnifying instrument called a colposcope. He may stain the woman's vulva, vagina, and cervix with acetic acid, a vinegar-type solution that makes the warts more easily seen. (A man may have this stain applied to his penis and scrotum.) A small portion of the growth (a biopsy) may be removed for laboratory testing if there is any question about its identity. No doctor would want to treat a growth as a mere wart when it might already be a cancer.

If a Pap smear has indicated precancerous (or cancerous) changes, a colposcopy is usually performed on the cervix. This involves staining the cervix with acetic acid for a few minutes and then magnifying the area with the colposcope. Small biopsies would then be taken to make certain that the HPV had not already caused cancer. If the growth *is* cancer, it must be treated aggressively—with radical surgery or radiation therapy.

If invasive cancer is not present, the cervix is usually either frozen or treated with the laser, or minor surgery is performed. These techniques can usually be done on an outpatient basis. If a Pap smear continues to be abnormal after the laser or freeze technique has been used, the entire procedure—from colposcopy on—is repeated.

There are many new techniques available for detecting the human papilloma virus. The virus will not grow in culture, so other tests are required for its detection. The Vira Pap HPV DNA Detection Kit is a method that can be used in the office to detect HPV. Although this test can show its presence, doctors are not sure how helpful this will be.

Even if there is HPV, no treatment is necessary if there are no warts or abnormalities of the cervix.

## How Are Venereal Warts Treated?

If venereal warts are present, podophyllin or trichloracetic acid is usually used to treat them. Multiple treatments are often necessary. If that is unsuccessful, freezing the warts, using the laser, or cutting away the warts can be tried. If these treatments do not work, injections with a drug called interferon may be administered. This is very expensive and requires multiple injections, but can often eliminate resistant warts. Venereal warts may disappear after the simplest treatment, but for some women, treatment can require years and thousands of dollars.

## What Are the Dangers of HPV Infection?

For men, the primary danger from this disease is cancer of the penis, although this is not common. When penile cancer occurs, it is almost always due to an HPV infection. If a man develops a wart-like growth on his penis or scrotum, he should get a diagnosis and treatment immediately.

The primary danger from HPV infection for women includes cancer of the cervix, vulva, or vagina, which is almost always caused by this virus. About 10 percent of women with cervical cancer will eventually develop cancer of the vulva. If the vulvar cancer is extensive, the entire vulvar area (labia majora and labia minora) must be removed. This is major surgery. (A study done in Connecticut shows that early cancer of the vulva in that state has *increased forty times during the past thirty years*.)

During pregnancy, venereal warts tend to proliferate quite rapidly. In addition, it has been found that children born to women who have HPV in their genital tracts may later develop laryngeal papillomata (throat warts). It is most likely that, as the baby is being born, it sucks in some of the mother's infectious vaginal secretions, causing the virus to start growing on the vocal cords. Surgery is necessary to remove these warts, and that can cause permanent scarring of the baby's vocal cords. This condition is a difficult medical problem for the child and its parents. Since the incidence of vocal-cord papilloma is relatively low, unless there are many active, growing venereal warts in the birth canal, most doctors do not recommend a cesarean section merely because an HPV infection has been diagnosed.

Thirty years ago, abnormal Pap smears that showed precancerous cells (dysplasia or cervical intraepithelial neoplasia) were very rare in women below the age of twenty-five. This is no longer the case. In a review of one million Pap smears obtained in Planned Parenthood Centers from 1981 to 1983, precancerous changes were found on the Pap smears of girls as young as fifteen. The average age of women with mildly abnormal Pap smears was 25.7, and the average age for those with invasive cancer was 31.9 (reported by Sadeghi and colleagues, *Cancer*, 61:2359-2361).

This markedly increased rate of precancerous findings in young women is believed to be a direct result of the generally increased sexual activity over the past few decades that exposes women to HPV infection at an earlier age than ever before. The trend has continued to the present.

Similarly, the Centers for Disease Control estimated that there has been a sixfold overall increase in HPV genital infections for men and women between the years 1966 and 1981. Experts say this infection has reached epidemic proportions. A report in *OB-GYN News* (vol. 24, no. 6) called genital warts the fastest-growing sexually transmitted disease in the United States. In an article recording a dialogue between authorities on HPV infections (Drs. Peter J. Lynch, Richard Reed, and Ralph M. Richart), Dr. Richart is quoted as saying, "I don't want to exaggerate the risk, but I think society needs to recognize that HPV (infection), under certain circumstances, *is the only sexually transmitted disease that commonly kills middle class American heterosexual women.*

The fact has been overlooked by everybody in the field" (italics added).

The same article states that HPV infections kill far more women each year than do HIV (AIDS) infections. According to Dr. Richart, 400 women die annually from AIDS, but 8,000 women die annually from HPV-associated genital cancers (cancers of the vulva, vagina, and cervix). He adds, "In my patients I perceive an excessive fear of AIDS, an absolute horror of herpes, but no real awareness of HPV."

It is very important for you to know about these infections, especially about the risk you are taking when you have intercourse outside of marriage, or have intercourse with anyone (including your spouse) who has venereal warts. Moreover, whatever your sexual history (and especially if you suspect that you have venereal warts or have been exposed to someone who has them), it is vital that you have regular gynecological examinations, including a yearly Pap smear. If either genital warts or precancerous cervical changes are discovered, these conditions must be promptly treated.

## Implications

HPV infection may be the most common sexually transmitted disease in the United States. Although chlamydia presently holds this record, studies are beginning to show that HPV infections may be even more prevalent. Further facts include:

1. HPV infections are the most rapidly increasing sexually transmitted disease and cannot be taken for granted. These infections are presently (1990) killing many more women than AIDS.

2. Genital HPV infection has a particular affinity for young women. When 796,337 Pap smears of women of all ages were evaluated, nearly one-fourth of the abnormal smears were from women between the ages of 15 and 19.

Most of these girls had had sexual intercourse before the age of 15, and more than half had had more than one partner.

3. Older women who have had multiple sex partners have a similar risk of developing precancerous and cancerous changes to the cervix from HPV.

4. The partner of a person with an HPV infection will contract the virus from 60 to 90 percent of the time.

5. The HPV can be carried undetected for days, months, and perhaps years, but the disease can be transmitted during this time. It is estimated that up to 30 percent of all sexually active women and men have this virus.

6. For a woman, HPV infection can involve multiple visits to a physician, colposcopies, biopsies, laser treatments, repeated Pap smears, etc.

All the worry and expense related to HPV infection can be avoided by following the basic guideline that sex is only for marriage. If neither partner in a mutually monogamous marriage has ever had sex with anyone else, HPV infection will not develop.

# AIDS

WHEN THE 1980s ushered in the AIDS epidemic, William, a practicing homosexual for many years, had already grown tired of his lifestyle—and the threat of AIDS was the incentive he needed to make a major change. William decided to go straight. But he decided too late, for he had already contracted AIDS.

Overcome with shock and grief, William related a sad and frightening tale to my physician friend, an infectious-disease specialist. Although William had not had sex with any men from 1984 to 1987, he did have sex with six women during those years. It is a fairly safe assumption that William had become infected with the human immuno-deficient virus—the cause of AIDS—during his homosexual days and had unknowingly become a carrier of this deadly disease. Each subsequent sexual partner was a potential victim.

Although William did not know what had happened to all of his female sexual partners, he did know that two were prostitutes and three had gotten married. Like ripples in a stream, William's legacy of death is probably even now spreading in ever widening circles.

The unsuspecting husbands of the three married women and the countless customers of the two prostitutes could now have AIDS. Furthermore, any *other* woman who subsequently had sex with one of these possibly infected men may also develop AIDS, years after William began this particular cycle of infection. The possibilities are endless.

Such disease networks go on and on. Whenever two people who are not virgins have sex, there is the chance that one (or both) of these people already has AIDS and/or is capable of transmitting it.

## What Is AIDS?

AIDS (Acquired Immune Deficiency Syndrome) is a viral infection caused by the human immunodeficiency virus (HIV). Former terms, including HTLV-III, the human T-cell lymphotrophic virus, and others, are no longer in general use.

---

**The HIV germ is 1000 times more complex than the herpes germ.**

---

HIV is a "retrovirus." It is selective, choosing the immune cells in a human body to attack. (Brain and spinal cord cells can also be damaged, however.) Once an HIV infection occurs, it spreads throughout the cells of the immune system, destroying them as it goes. The human immunodeficiency virus is one of the most variable viruses known. Over 150 strains have already been identified.

Although most people (including some physicians) refer to those who are HIV-infected as having AIDS, that is not technically correct. While the potential for developing full-blown AIDS exists in HIV-infected individuals—and the disease will ultimately develop—the term *AIDS* is not truly applicable until the "silent" period is passed. At that point, when the immune system has been severely damaged, opportunistic infections that would otherwise not be a problem become life threatening. As these begin to occur in an HIV-infected individual, he or she is said to have AIDS.

The term *HIV-positive* is used for anyone who has been infected with HIV. Once this infection occurs, a person is infected and contagious for life. Not only can future sexual partners contract AIDS from this person, but also his or her blood can infect others through breaks in the skin, shared drug needles, and transfusions.

However, I will use "HIV-infected" throughout this chapter to refer to a person who has been *infected* with the AIDS virus, whether or not the disease symptoms are present. Such a person is considered as contagious to others as if the infection were already "mature." *And, short of a miracle, he or she will develop AIDS and eventually die from it.*

A person who is HIV-positive may feel perfectly healthy and be unaware of carrying the AIDS virus. Even a blood test can give a false sense of security, since it may fail to show positive from months to years after infection. *In fact, it may take longer than that.* An Associated Press news release from Boston (quoted in *Houston Post* June 1, 1989) stated that people at high risk of developing AIDS may silently harbor the AIDS virus *for years,* while standard blood tests show them to be free of infection (though this rarely happens). A study conducted by Dr. David T. Imagawa of the University of California at Los Angeles and published in the *New England Journal of Medicine* (June 1, 1989) revealed that HIV can permanently insert itself into the genes of blood cells but stay "hidden," so that the body does not produce antibodies for three years—and perhaps much longer—after the initial infection.

Dr. William A. Haseltine of Dana-Farber Cancer Institute in Boston, an AIDS expert familiar with Dr. Imagawa's research, cautioned that the discovery "raises the sobering possibility that people with silent infections may pass on the virus through blood and organ donations."

AIDS is spread by the exchange of HIV-infected body fluids: blood and blood products and semen (and possibly saliva and even tears). Principal transmission is through intimate sexual contact or through the use of contaminated I.V. needles in the drug-use population. Before mandatory testing was instituted for blood-bank reserves, hemophiliacs were at great risk from receiving transfusions of HIV-infected blood. In addition, dental professionals now routinely wear rubber gloves since—if even a minor cut were present on their hands—they would be at risk from any AIDS virus that might be present in the blood of patients with periodontal (gum) disease or those requiring dental surgery.

AIDS has not been proven to be spread in restaurants, by mosquitoes, by hugging, by toilet seats, by eating utensils, by hairdressers, or by shaking hands. *To be transmissible, the AIDS virus needs the warmth and moist surfaces available in intimate contact or the commingling of blood.*

A report released in March 1989 by the Texas Department of Health revealed some startling statistics. The study (prepared by University of Texas researchers Demetri Vacalis, Ph.D., Pamela J. Shoemaker, Ph.D., and Alfred McAlister, Ph.D.) indicated that:

1. Most Texans did not know the signs and symptoms of AIDS.

2. One-sixth of the population was unaware that healthy-appearing people can be a source of HIV infection.

3. A majority of Texans stated their belief that AIDS was a result of a breakdown of traditional values.

4. Subjects who attended religious services most often were less likely to have had multiple sex partners or to have had sex with prostitutes. The most sexually active group was the 18- to 24-year-old group, with blacks more likely to report multiple sex partners than Hispanics or Anglos.

5. Those considered "at risk" through sexual activity were those who had been sexually active and either (a) had more than one sexual partner in the past year, or (b) had been in a mutually faithful relationship for less than seven years, prior to which they had been sexually active.

6. Only half of the "at risk" respondents to the survey had used a condom in the past year, and only 32 percent of that half had the condom in place before the first genital contact was made.

## What Is the Course of AIDS Infection?

The progression of AIDS usually follows a typical course. Within four to eight weeks after contracting HIV, a mild mononucleosis-like infection appears. This does not last long and usually disappears completely.

Within a year of the initial infection, a blood test is usually positive for antibodies to HIV. Although this can happen as early as six weeks after infection, it can take as long as three years or even longer. An individual with HIV is considered contagious from the time of the initial infection—even before a blood test is positive.

Because of the undetectable presence of HIV for such a variable period of time, blood banks have found it difficult to eliminate all risks of transfusions. A further complication to this problem is the identification of the HIV-2 strain of AIDS. Although most AIDS victims in the United States have HIV-1, at least two cases of HIV-2 infection have been identified in this country. According to a Reuter News Service release (*Houston Post*, May 1989), HIV-2 was first identified in West Africa in 1985. Since then, it has spread rapidly through Africa and Europe. *At the present time, there is no standard blood test to identify this virus, making it possible for the HIV-2 virus to be transmitted through blood transfusion and organ donations.*

HIV-infected persons often develop enlarged lymph nodes, usually in the back of the neck and under the arms.

(Approximately 50 percent develop enlarged lymph nodes somewhere in their bodies.) Some people have intermittent fever, weight loss, occasional diarrhea, candida mouth infections, and shingles as the immune deficiency from HIV progresses.

Once the immune system is destroyed or deficient, three types of major problems may develop. Certain "opportunistic" infections that would not normally infect a healthy person take advantage of the immunodeficiency to invade the body. These include pneumocystis pneumonia, toxoplasmosis, and cytomegalovirus infections, among others.

Another AIDS-related problem that can develop is that of malignancies that do not usually occur in young, otherwise healthy individuals. These include non-Hodgkin's lymphoma and Kaposi's sarcoma. Finally, AIDS encephalitis, with dementia, is a possibility.

Within a year of the development of these AIDS symptoms, 50 percent of the victims die. Within three years, the mortality rate is 90 percent.

## Can I Be HIV Infected Without Knowing It?

It is indeed possible to be infected with HIV and not know it. Evidence suggests that the incubation period (length of time from exposure to onset of symptoms) can range from a few months to several years. Thus, the only way to know for sure if you are infected and/or carrying the disease is by undergoing the testing procedures outlined below.

## Can My Sexual Partner Have HIV Without My Knowing It?

It is highly unlikely that you would know if your sexual partner is carrying the virus unless he has full-blown AIDS. There are two reasons for this. First, your partner may not have any idea he is infected for months or years after infection (see preceding question). Second, he may know (or suspect) infection and not tell you.

There are many tragic stories of people who had intercourse with individuals who blatantly ignored suspicious symptoms or an HIV positive blood test and continued having sexual relations. Perhaps this is not too hard to understand. If you know you are HIV infected, you realize that for the rest of your life you should be celibate. If you are not, you will probably pass this deadly disease to your sexual partner, whether in or out of marriage. Facing the fact that sexual abstinence is the only right course for the remainder of one's life is an additional heavy burden for anyone to bear.

The sad fact is that *anyone* who has ever had sex outside a marriage relationship could be HIV infected, transmitting it to future sexual partners. To date, no effective vaccine against AIDS has been developed. And no so-called protective device is 100 percent fail-proof!

## How Is HIV Diagnosed?

The ELISA blood test (enzyme-linked immunosorbent assay) is the best screening test for HIV at the present time. If the ELISA test is positive twice, a Western Blot test is done to confirm the accuracy of the ELISA. This eliminates any false-positive ELISA tests and thus identifies an individual who is infected or carrying the virus.

A new antigen test will soon be released by the FDA. This measures virus particles in the blood and will help doctors determine the degree of activity of HIV in an infected person.

## What Is the Treatment for AIDS?

There is no known cure for AIDS, and HIV-infected individuals will probably develop AIDS and eventually die from its effects. AZT (zidovudine) is a drug that is helpful in suppressing viral activity, but it is not a cure. Worldwide research continues to seek both further treatment methods and a preventive vaccine.

Although AIDS is essentially a death sentence, a person with AIDS can determine to lead a useful life and make the most of his or her remaining time, just as victims of other terminal illnesses do. It would seem that part of this usefulness should be in taking responsibility for not infecting others and in helping to educate their friends and society in general of the dangers of indulging in activities that places one at high risk for contracting AIDS.

An AIDS victim is no less a person and is still capable of giving and receiving love in many meaningful ways. Since this disease is emotionally and physically devastating, we should reach out to all of its sufferers with compassion and help them to bear their burden.

## What Are the Dangers of AIDS?

The obvious dangers of AIDS are increasing debilitation and death. Another, but not so well-known, danger is to the children born to HIV-infected mothers. About 30 percent of these babies are born with HIV infection, and very few of them live more than a few years.

## Implications

In spite of increased publicity and available information, AIDS is still spreading rapidly in our society. It is estimated that the number of people with AIDS is doubling every 2.8 years. Many of the statistics regarding AIDS are startling:

1. As with most other sexually transmitted diseases, AIDS seems to be increasing especially rapidly in the teenage population. Dr. Karen Hein of the Medical College of Virginia in Richmond said, "A much-feared heterosexual wave of AIDS has happened, and is happening, among teenagers." (*OB/GYN News,* vol. 23, no. 13, July 1988).

According to Dr. Hein, some studies indicate that 20 percent of all HIV-infected people became infected as teenagers.

2. Among teenagers, there are just as many females as males who are HIV-infected, showing that HIV is a heterosexual disease; in adult groups, more men than women have the virus.

3. Dr. Allen Guinan of the Centers for Disease Control in Atlanta showed that women accounted for 10 percent of all AIDS cases in 1988, an increase of more than 40 percent from 1987 (*OB/GYN News*, Feb. 1988). AIDS is the leading killer of women in the 25-34 age group in New York City. In 1981, women comprised only 3 percent of AIDS cases in the United States. Heterosexual women are at least four times more likely than heterosexual men to acquire AIDS through heterosexual intercourse.

4. One of the big myths of AIDS is that it is contracted from "kinky" sex. AIDS, however, is not so selective. It is transmissible through "normal" penile/vaginal intercourse.

5. There is no "safe sex" when one partner has AIDS. In one study it was found that when couples had intercourse without protection, thirteen out of sixteen uninfected partners became infected. If couples used condoms, two out of twelve (17 percent) became infected during the short period of the study. And these were couples in which the uninfected partner knew that his/her partner had AIDS and was being excruciatingly careful about using so-called protective measures.

6. According to Dr. Robert Redfield, an infectious disease expert with Walter Reed Army Hospital in Washington, it is estimated that in ten years, one in 200 males in our country and one in 400 females will be HIV-positive.

7. One in two hundred teenagers who graduate from high school in Washington, D.C., is infected with HIV. And in New York, 1 in 112 women delivering babies is HIV-positive. (In some areas of Africa, where AIDS has been present longer than it has in the U.S., one in five women delivering babies is HIV-positive.)

8. The statistics from Africa are quite frightening because they could foreshadow what might happen in the United States. A study reported in the *Journal of the American Medical Association* (Dec. 1988) on blood tests of all patients in a group of fifteen hospitals in Uganda during a one-week period found that 42 percent were HIV-positive.

9. AIDS is alarmingly present in our colleges. A CDC study reported in *American Medical Association News* (June 2, 1990) showed that 2 in 1,000 college students test positive for AIDS.

10. The risk of infection with a sexually transmitted disease climbs as the number of persons with whom a person has had intercourse increases. *The Journal of the American Medical Association* (Oct. 1988) stated that a sizable percentage of young, never-married men reported more than ten partners during the previous twelve months. A woman who has intercourse with one of those men should consider the fact that, in effect, she is having sex with all the people with whom her partner has ever had sex.

11. The *American Medical News* (March 18, 1988) reported that a new HIV (HIV-2) has been found in the United States for the first time. Current blood-screening techniques will not detect the HIV-2. Although most AIDS in the United States is thought to be caused by the HIV-1, the HIV-2 will no doubt continue to spread, necessitating the developing of new screening tests for blood banks.

Dr. Roger W. Enlow, an AIDS expert, said in 1983, "We will have the answer [to AIDS] within two years" (*American Medical Association News*, August 5, 1983). What a naive statement! This exemplifies the wishful thinking that most people adopt in regard to *any* sexually transmitted disease. And the AIDS virus is much more complicated than most viruses that affect humans. A significant number of experts now feel that there may *never* be a vaccine effective against HIV, and that it will be years before a cure is discovered, if ever.

Once again I have good news. You don't need to worry about HIV if you and the person you marry never had sex before marriage, maintain a monogamous relationship once married, never have used or use I.V. drugs, and have never had a blood transfusion.

# 14

# Hepatitis B

JOHN, ALEX, AND JEFF lived in the same small area of a moderate-sized town. Although they had known each other in high school, they had gone their separate ways after graduation. When all three young men developed acute cases of hepatitis B between May and July of the following year, it became clear that these three heterosexual men had more in common than the same high school. They had all had sexual relations with the same woman.

They weren't the only ones. A health-department check revealed that this woman had engaged in intercourse with eight different men in a six-month period of time. Contact was made with only two other of the eight men, neither of whom had contracted hepatitis B. But it is likely that at least one or two of the men the department was unable to locate developed the disease. These men may now be transmitting hepatitis B to their sexual partners.

One of them could be you, or someone you know.

## What Is Hepatitis B?

Although it was only fifteen years ago that hepatitis B was first thought to be sexually transmitted, it is now known to be one of the most common STDs in the world. Hepatitis B is caused by a virus that is transmissible through body fluids—blood and blood-derived products, semen and vaginal fluids, and saliva. This virus basically affects functioning of the liver, often causing damage that is severe enough to be fatal.

As with AIDS, there are other ways to transmit the disease than through sexual intercourse. Blood transfusions and any other exchange of body fluids (such as getting infected blood onto a break in the skin or using contaminated I.V. needles) can also cause a hepatitis B infection.

## Can I Have Hepatitis B Without Knowing It?

Not only can you have hepatitis B without being aware of it, but you can also be a chronic carrier of the disease for years without knowing it. If you *are* a carrier, you may feel no ill effects right now (or have already recovered from them), but for the rest of your life you might infect those with whom you have sex. In addition, you might transmit the disease to others through blood donations or other fluid exchange.

## Can My Sexual Partner Have Hepatitis B Without My Knowing It?

Because hepatitis B has either no symptoms or relatively unobscure symptoms, you and your sexual partner may be unaware that he either has hepatitis B or is a carrier of the disease.

## How Is Hepatitis B Diagnosed?

Hepatitis B is diagnosed by a blood test that would be ordered if a person has the typical symptoms of hepatitis.

These include yellowing of the skin and whites of the eyes (jaundice), tiredness, nausea, dark urine and gray-colored stools. However, sometimes the disease produces few symptoms or none at all. Experts advise all pregnant women to have a blood test for hepatitis B—because they can have the disease and pass it on to their babies without knowing it.

## How Is Hepatitis B Treated?

There is no known cure for hepatitis B. As with other forms of hepatitis, the treatment for hepatitis B is non-specific, supportive care, which includes rest as a primary part of the regimen. Most people recover from the infection, but some become carriers and have the infection for years with no symptoms.

## Is Hepatitis B Dangerous?

The primary dangers of hepatitis B are severe liver damage and the possibility of passing on the disease to others, especially one's sexual partners. Ten percent of people who contract hepatitis B will develop a persistent infection that can have extremely dangerous effects, including cancer of the liver and cirrhosis.

A person who becomes a chronic carrier can pass the disease to anyone with whom he or she has sex. Carriers can also pass it to anyone who comes in contact with their bodily secretions or blood. It is not uncommon for health-care professionals—dentists, dental hygienists, obstetricians, surgeons, and others—to contract hepatitis B from their patients. Then they themselves may become carriers and pass it on to other patients. Because of this, many people who are at risk for acquiring hepatitis B on the job have had themselves immunized against hepatitis B. (I have done this, and so have my nurses. I highly recommend it for anyone who might come in contact with patients' blood.) In addition, anyone who suspects that he or she has been exposed to hepatitis B virus (through sexual activity with an infected partner, for example) should promptly consult a physician, since immunoglobulin may provide some protection, as will hepatitis B vaccine.

As previously mentioned, an infected pregnant woman can transmit a hepatitis B infection to her baby, possibly making the child a carrier for life. Even worse, 40 to 50 percent of these children will develop cancer of the liver. Many of the others will have severe liver disease. A woman who suspects she might have hepatitis should have a blood test to determine whether that is the case. As a matter of fact, many obstetricians order this routinely for their pregnant patients. If she does have the disease, her baby will receive immunoglobulin at birth, followed by a series of vaccine injections in the hope of providing long-lasting immunity.

## Implications

One of the most important aspects of this sexually transmitted disease was reported in the *Journal of the American Medical Association* (Sept. 12, 1986). Dr. Schreeder's studies of university students showed that a person who has had fewer than ten sexual partners has a relatively low risk of getting hepatitis B. A history of more than ten partners presents a huge increase in the possibility of contracting this infection.

Of course, the safest course is to have no sexual intercourse until marriage. But a person who has had multiple sex partners over a period of time, *and who has not yet developed hepatitis B, AIDS, or other sexually transmitted disease, should stop those sexual practices now if he or she wants to stay healthy.*

# 15

# Vaginitis

MARY ALICE WAS sick and tired of the hassles of dealing with her recurring vaginal discharge. She was annoyed over the odor, weary of the itching, and unhappy about spending her hard-earned money on panty liners, feminine-hygiene sprays, and douche solutions, none of which solved the problem.

Mary Alice finally got exasperated enough to see her doctor—and was shocked to learn that the "innocent" discharge that she thought was normal for all women was caused by a sexually transmitted disease. Having to tell her current boyfriend about the infection so that he, too, could be treated was embarrassing, and the office call and treatment measures made new inroads on her already-tight budget.

Mary Alice recovered. And got a new boyfriend. And promptly got another infection.

Mary Alice should have been told the complete facts: that staying with one partner would solve the problem of those aggravating vaginal infections, assuming that he, too, was faithful.

Perhaps her doctor should have told her about the dramatic contrast in disease rates between women who change sexual partners, even occasionally, and those who stay with one man for years in a stable marriage relationship. The latter is almost never seen in a doctor's office for any type of vaginal infection except candida (commonly known as monilia or yeast infection).

## What Is Vaginitis?

There are basically two types of what is known as "vaginitis." One, trichomoniasis is an infection caused by a protozoan *Trichomonas vaginalis*. Except in rare cases, this parasite is spread only by sexual intercourse, making it a true sexually transmitted disease.

Trichomonal vaginitis causes a vaginal discharge and itching of the vulva. The itching can be quite intolerable, and it is often this discomfort that forces a woman to see a physician. Tenderness and burning of the vulva frequently accompany the infection, often leading to pain with intercourse.

Although men who have contracted this infection occasionally have a discharge from the penis, they usually have no other symptoms. Very rarely they may have occasional slight burning with urination.

Since being recognized as a sexually transmitted disease, trichomoniasis is now known to be one of the most common STDs in the world. For example, 90 percent of prostitutes have this infection at one time or another.

*Gardnerella vaginalis* (or *Hemophilus vaginalis*) is a bacterium that causes another type of vaginitis. A woman with this infection will have a vaginal discharge that may initially be misinterpreted as only heavy vaginal secretions. The most bothersome symptom of the discharge, aside from stained underwear, is the fishy odor. There may also be a very mild burning and itching in the vaginal area.

Infected men usually have no symptoms of Gardnerella.

Gardnerella vaginitis is almost invariably sexually transmitted and is present in 10 to 20 percent of women of reproductive age.

## Can I Have Vaginitis Without Knowing It?

Both Trichomonas and Gardnerella organisms can be present in the vagina for weeks or even months before symptoms are present, but trichomoniasis is the most likely of the two to remain hidden. A woman with Gardnerella will usually notice a change in vaginal secretions within five to ten days of being infected.

## Can My Sexual Partner Have Trichomonas or Gardnerella Infections Without My Knowing It?

Both men and women can carry the Trichomonas or Gardnerella organisms for years without knowing it. However, even without symptoms, it can be passed to another person during sexual intercourse.

## How Is Vaginitis Diagnosed?

If a doctor examines a patient who has a watery vaginal discharge and itching, he or she may notice that the discharge is frothy and slightly green. In that case, on looking at the secretions under the microscope, the doctor will usually see Trichomonas protozoa moving around.

On the other hand, when a doctor examines a patient who has a vaginal discharge accompanied by odor, the secretions will often be somewhat gray-colored and slightly creamy. Then, microscopic examination may reveal "clue cells"—normal vaginal cells that have the Gardnerella organism "stuck" to them. The vaginal cells will appear to have hundreds of small knots growing out of them. This is a typical finding with Gardnerella vaginitis.

## What Is the Treatment for Trichomonas and Gardnerella?

Treatment for both these vaginal infections is a drug called metronidazole, commonly known as Flagyl. It comes in both pill form and as an injectable medication and is obtained only by prescription. The pill form is used for the treatment of vaginitis. (The injectable form is used in patients hospitalized for serious infections that are un-related to vaginitis.) When a standard dose of Flagyl is used for vaginitis, the infection does not always clear up promptly. A second, larger dose of Flagyl is then pre-scribed. Even then the infection may be resistant to treat-ment. Though not dangerous, occasionally these infections can be very tenacious.

The partner of a woman with vaginitis must also be treated to prevent possible re-infection. It is recommended that sexual intercourse be avoided during the period of infection and treatment.

## What Are the Dangers of Vaginitis?

Neither trichomoniasis nor Gardnerella is considered a dangerous infection, but they are both exceedingly irritat-ing as well as aesthetically unpleasant.

## Implications

It is important for a woman with vaginitis to realize that the same sexual partner from whom she contracted those organisms may also harbor other, more dangerous diseases. Chlamydia, gonorrhea, syphilis, or any of the other sexually transmitted diseases may accompany Trichomonas or Gardnerella vaginitis. Because of the dan-ger of multiple infections, a woman may want to request examinations by her doctor for other sexually transmitted diseases.

I have discussed two causes of vaginitis. We gynecologists are seeing more and more women with exceedingly persistent vaginitis in spite of standard therapy. It has now been shown that an HPV infection at the entrance to the vagina (genital warts) can make these tissues very sore and tender for months. I believe we will find that other sexually transmitted organisms are complicating the treatment of persistent vaginitis in women who continue to change sexual partners. We almost never see persistent vaginitis in married women if both husband and wife are faithful to each other.

Ask women who have suffered it—a clean vagina with freedom from discharge, itch, and odor is another good reason to have sex only with one man for a lifetime.

# 16

# Other Sexually
# Transmitted Diseases

ALICIA, ONE OF our city's most socially prominent women, didn't consider herself promiscuous. She changed sexual partners "only once in a while," although I had warned her several years ago of the probability of acquiring a sexually transmitted disease in a nonmonogamous lifestyle. Alicia didn't think it could happen to her, however.

When she came to my office for her annual checkup this year, Alicia mentioned, offhandedly, that she must be allergic to her bubble bath or detergent, because she was experiencing persistent pubic itching. I immediately suspected pubic lice, and when I examined her found the characteristic "nits"—the eggs that the lice lay on the pubic hair— confirming my suspicion.

Alicia was amazed and embarrassed. I didn't say, "I told you so!" (I didn't even think it.) But I *had* told her so, and she could have avoided this traumatic experience if she had listened.

An infestation of pubic lice is only one of several sexually transmitted diseases not yet discussed in this book. Because these remaining few conditions either do not cause the serious problems that many of the previously discussed diseases do, or they are relatively uncommon, I will discuss them only briefly in this final chapter.

## Pubic Lice (Crabs)

Pubic lice are commonly known as "crabs." Visible to the naked eye, these tiny but bothersome creatures cause intense itching and irritation of the pubic skin. The inevitable scratching causes small sores that ooze pus.

Pubic lice are most frequently passed by direct contact with the pubic hair of an infected person during intercourse or other physical intimacy. These organisms can also be transmitted from the clothing or bed sheets of an infected person.

Pediculosis is the general term used for lice infestation. Pubic lice are not the same as head lice. Generally, head lice infect only the hair of the head, while pubic lice infect only the hair of the pubis. (Body lice, still another variety, are more medically serious because of certain diseases they carry.)

An infestation of pubic lice is not dangerous. Because of the availability of effective treatment, it is of no real consequence except that it can be spread sexually and is quite irritating while it is present.

It is possible for either you or your partner to have pubic lice without the other knowing it, since some people experience no symptoms, at least for some time.

If you suspect that you have "crabs," your doctor will examine your pubic hair carefully. If the pubic lice are present, the parasites and/or the nits will be visible, clinging to the hair close to the skin.

Your doctor will write a prescription for a medicated shampoo to kill this parasite and will suggest that you wash all bedclothes, towels, and undergarments in hot water so that reinfestation will not occur.

## Molluscum Contagiosum

Molluscum contagiosum is a skin disease caused by a virus. This virus is a mildly contagious poxvirus, and its effect is limited to the skin. It is transmitted through both sexual and nonsexual contact.

The infection produces bumps on the skin that are skin-colored, slightly raised, and somewhat waxy-looking. These lesions have a slight indention in the center, and may occur singly or in groups. The usual size of the Molluscum contagiosum lesion is about an eighth of an inch across. Occasionally, these bumps are "pedunculated"—protruding from the skin like a small tick.

Until 1977, Molluscum contagiosum was not regarded as a sexually transmitted disease. Because of this, some physicians are not aware of its relationship to sexual activity. If you have been found to have this infection, be sure your sexual partner also gets examined and treated.

After contact with a person who has this virus, growths may not be seen for several weeks or months. When they do develop, you will see them as bumps on the surface of the lower abdomen, the pubic area, the inner thighs, or the external genitalia. These lesions do not hurt (they may itch slightly) and are not dangerous. There may be only one or there may be several.

Both you and your partner can have Molluscum contagiosum without being initially aware of it. The bumps can be mistaken for ordinary pimples, even by a doctor. Most gynecologists are able to identify this infection by sight.

Molluscum contagiosum usually does not clear up spontaneously, but it can. Usually the doctor must treat it by scraping out the small, hard, white core of each of the growths. This usually cures the problem. If the growths recur, your doctor may use cautery or trichloracetic acid after scraping them again.

## Scabies

Scabies is a skin disease that causes intense itching. A fairly common infection, it accounts for 2 to 3 percent of all patients seen by dermatologists during the past few years.

Scabies is caused by a mite (*Sarcoptes scabiei*), a parasite of the skin. The mite burrows into the skin and forms a small, tortuous channel just under the surface. Its path can be seen with a magnifying glass. Scabies mites burrow into soft skin of the body, such as skin folds, the penis, the scrotum, finger webs, wrists, elbows, nipples, umbilicus, buttocks, and insteps.

Scabies is transmitted from one person to another by skin-to-skin contact. Transmission is not necessarily sexual and can occur through bedclothes or undergarments only if they have been contaminated immediately beforehand.

Scabies is not dangerous, but it is very bothersome. If the skin becomes badly irritated from scratching, impetigo (a bacterial infection) can develop. This secondary infection, if neglected, can lead to glomerulonephritis, a kidney disease.

You can have scabies and not be aware that it was spread by close contact, possibly sexual. A person who showers regularly and stays clean may have itching in only a small area, such as the umbilicus, and not realize the cause of the problem.

Scabies is diagnosed by looking at the area of itching with a magnifying instrument and discovering the burrowing channels. A doctor may scrape the skin of the burrow superficially and be able to see the parasite itself.

Treatment for scabies consists of applying a specific drug, such as Lindane, to all areas of the body except the head. The body should be thoroughly washed after eight hours and a change made to fresh clothing. (This treatment is not recommended for pregnant women and lactating mothers.)

All members of the family should be treated, as well as anyone else who has had close body contact with infected individuals.

## Chancroid, Lymphogranuloma Venereum (LGV), and Granuloma Inguinale (GI)

The Texas Department of Health has produced a small booklet called *Venereal Disease* that says of these three diseases:

Each is caused by a different organism. These diseases are occasionally found in Texas (i.e., 66 cases were reported in 1976). However, they are much more frequently seen in warm, tropic, and sub-tropical climates and in populations with low standards of hygiene.

Chancroid, GI, and LGV are highly dangerous and destructive diseases causing the loss of vital tissue in the reproductive organs, gross enlargement of the sex organs, stricture of the intestines and rectum, obstruction of the anus, even death.

Symptoms of these diseases are quite apparent: tender lesions breaking down into painful ulcers, spreading over the genital area or skin surface of the stomach, groin, and thighs; bumps turn into raw, oozing masses of tissue, and slow-healing lesions; a lesion with inflammatory swelling in the groin and accompanying fever, aches, and joint pains. These symptoms usually motivate an infected individual to seek a physician rather quickly.

It is hardly possible that either you or your sexual partner could have one of these three STDs and be unaware of it. Both chancroid and granuloma inguinale produce sores and ulcers of the genital area. Anyone who has these symptoms will certainly be aware of them.

Lymphogranuloma venereum, however, primarily causes infection of the colon. A person would not necessarily suspect a venereal disease in this case.

Ulcers in the genital area, enlarged lymph nodes without visible sores in the genital area, or diarrhea with blood and pus from the rectum, all indicate the possibility of sexually transmitted disease. If you or your sexual partner has these symptoms, a physician should be consulted immediately.

Chancroid, LGV, and GI are fairly rare infections, and a doctor not familiar with STDs might not make the correct diagnosis. If you suspect the possibility of having one of these diseases, and your doctor is not sure what is causing the problem, it would be wise to consult a dermatologist or a city or state health-department clinic. They are the experts in diagnosing these types of diseases.

Fortunately, all three of these diseases generally respond quite well to antibiotics. If too much tissue has been destroyed because of neglect and delay in seeking treatment, however, resultant scarring can cause lingering medical problems.

As with other STDs, the number of people in the United States with these diseases is increasing. For example, 3,416 cases of chancroid were reported in 1986, the largest number since 1952. The number of cases for the first six months of 1987 increased 42 percent over the same period of 1986 (reported in *Medical Aspects of Human Sexuality,* April 1989).

## Other Diseases That Can Be Spread Sexually

Although there are more than thirty diseases that can be passed sexually, not all of them are initially contracted in this way. For example, a woman may develop a vaginal Candida infection (overabundance of yeast or fungus) that has nothing whatever to do with sexual intercourse. (Many women carry the *Candida albicans* organism all the time.) The Candida infection, also known as monilia, can be passed to a sexual partner, however, causing itching and irritation of the man's penis. If the woman has *her* infection treated, but the man does not, he can re-infect her, making the disease, in effect, sexually transmitted. This does commonly occur in marriages, even when both partners are faithful to each other.

There are a number of infections of this type. Some diseases that may not *initially* be sexually contracted, but can be sexually transmitted, are the following:

1. *Cytomegalovirus infections (CMV).* This disease, caused by a virus from the herpes group, can be passed by blood transfusions, intimate contact, and sexual intercourse. It is very common in homosexual men and is strongly associated with men and women who have multiple sexual partners. (It can be dangerous in newborns infected by the mother.)

2. *Amebiasis.* This infection causes diarrhea and other intestinal problems. The disease is much more common in tropical regions than in the United States. Although this parasitic infection is not considered a sexually transmitted disease, it can be transmitted in this way. Complications may involve the liver.

3. *Giardiasis.* Like amebiasis, this parasitic infection can cause diarrhea and, while not specifically an STD, it can definitely be passed sexually.

4. *Group B Beta hemolytic streptococcal infection.* While not considered an STD, this infection can be passed sexually. It rarely hurts the man or woman who becomes infected, but it is dangerous to newborn babies who pick up the infection in the mother's birth canal. This germ is common and has been found in as many as 20 percent of all women.

5. *Mycoplasma infections.* These common infections can be found in from 7 to 20 percent of all people. While they do not harm men, they are associated with infertility and spontaneous abortion.

6. *Shigella and Salmonella.* These two bacterial infections can cause severe diarrhea and can be passed from person to person, with or without sexual intercourse.

7. *Epstein-Barr virus.* This infection, which can cause a person to be chronically ill, was just recently shown to be spread sexually.

There are a number of other much less common infections that are not sexual in origin but can be passed sexually. Each year there seem to be additions to the list of organisms that can be transmitted sexually.

Write to
**Baker Book House**
P.O. Box 6287
Grand Rapids, MI 49516

for information regarding
a set of transparencies
that highlight facts
presented in
*SAFE SEX*